The Expatriate Dilemma

*How to Relocate
and Compensate
U.S. Employees
Assigned Overseas*

The Expatriate Dilemma

*How to Relocate
and Compensate
U.S. Employees
Assigned Overseas*

Stan W. Frith

Nelson-Hall nh Chicago

Library of Congress Cataloging in Publication Data

Frith, Stan W.
  The expatriate dilemma.

  Includes index.
  1. Americans in foreign countries—Employment.
2. International business enterprises—Personnel
management.   I.   Title.
HF5549.5.E45F74   658.3′83   81–2740
ISBN 0–88229–701–5   AACR2

Manufactured in the United States of America

10   9   8   7   6   5   4   3   2   1

*Dedicated to wife Gillian
and sons Jason and Rory*

Contents

Acknowledgments

IN RESEARCHING AND writing this book, I have drawn on the knowledge, experience, and skill of my friend and colleague Burgess Buchanan, who used his background and experience to clarify, correct and in some cases rewrite my material. Also, Richard Wilson of Arthur Young & Company, for critiquing the section on Federal income tax rules applicable to U.S. expatriates. Sincere thanks are also due to Joanne Galley, my secretary, who spent innumerable evenings deciphering my handwriting and typing the manuscript.

Also, of course, we should not forget all those expatriates who, when asked how they spend their income, answer:

"About 30 percent on accommodation, 30 percent on clothing, 40 percent for goods and services, and 20 percent for amusement."

"But that totals 120 percent," you argue.

True or false, real or imagined, this is *The Expatriate Dilemma!*

Introduction

IN RECENT YEARS, many multinational corporations have invested hundreds of thousands of dollars researching, developing and continually updating methods for calculating expatriate compensation. Varied attempts have been made to find the ultimate foreign service compensation equation which reconciles the continual perturbations in rates of inflation with currency fluctuations. Because the optimum solution for each company depends on the correct permutation from a seemingly endless matrix of parameters and variables, this is no easy task.

Any change in an individual's job function, responsibility, or financial condition, whether the result of a transfer, a promotion, or, as in this text, an expatriate assignment, involves numerous uncertainties, discomforts, and anxieties. The most common uncertainty is about income, especially with the expatriate compensation "package." The most common discomforts are the cultural changes, language barriers, and isolation of being away from home. The most common anxieties involve the necessity of abandoning old social ties and forming new ones. All of these intangible considerations represent what the individual thinks he may be asked to sacrifice in exchange for agreeing to the company's request to "go foreign."

It would be easy to argue that no monetary price can be set on intangibles such as anxiety or uncertainty, but that really depends on the individual's values. In reality, most people do have a price, and, while there is nothing necessarily dishonorable or reprehensible about that, an international compensation administrator is faced with a monumental task in formulating a sufficiently liberal increment to offset prospective expatriate anxieties while at the same time protecting the financial goals of the foreign operation. The cost of managing an international business is already greater than a domestic business. Investment stakes are high, and mistakes are costly—and so are expatriates, as we will see later.

The advent of the European Common Market and the ameliorative efforts of the underdeveloped countries, along with the shrinking of distances and faster communication, have given rise to an increasing number of international or multinational corporations. The resultant expatriate explosion has brought with it a conglomeration of calculations, computations, formulas and equations all aimed at rationalizing the interrelationship between inflation and exchange rates vis-à-vis foreign service compensation.

To understand expatriate compensation and the various theories and techniques the compensation administrator may employ in handling his work, it is necessary to comprehend not only the theoretical bases and mechanics of the expatriate package, but also that in recent years governments have tended to enact more and more regulations affecting expatriates which a company cannot disregard without incurring penalties.

This book is designed to bring the elements of expatriate administration into sharp focus, identify critical problems, and outline a practical program to increase the expatriate's contribution to corporate profits. The aim has been to make the book useful not only to expatriate compensation administrators, but also to financial analysts, to managers, and to expatriates themselves.

The word "panacea" in regard to expatriate compensation and administration is a euphemism—properly in quotation marks. However, insofar as possible, in a field that touches on so many different parameters and variables, I have tried to provide a concise reference collection of the more important programs and procedures being used by multinational corporations today.

The views and ideas expressed in this book are my own, based on experiences I have gathered in recent years when formulating corporate policies for expatriates. I have avoided in-depth discussion on taxation, pension funds, and other very specialized activities, for fear that they might have made this book intolerably complex and long. Compensation is an integrated activity, but it is easier to comprehend when broken down into its component parts. The following chapters attempt to do just that.

Note: For simplicity's sake, I have used "man" and "his" throughout this book to stand for "man or woman" and "his or hers."

Chapter 1

Some Basic Questions and Answers

● *What is an expatriate?*

An expatriate could be defined as an American citizen or resident alien who relocates from the United States to work for the company in an overseas location for a contracted period of time, usually in excess of one year.

● *Are there different types of expatriates?*

Yes, basically there are two. In certain industries it is desirable to have expatriates who are willing to move from country to country for an indeterminate period of time. Often referred to as "career expatriates" or "globalists," these individuals become international nomads and spend years traveling the world with little or no desire to return to their country of origin; at least not in the short term. Usually single, with few ties or commitments, these globe-trotters are exceedingly valuable to those companies where the nature of the business demands mobility, flexibility and rugged individualism. The other type are "conventional expatriates," or "standard expatriates," those individuals whose assignment overseas is for a shorter period of time (usually two to four years) and who retain close ties with their country of origin. These individuals are often sent on single assignments to set up an installation, fix a specific problem, or train local staff; on completion of the project, they return promptly to their country of origin.

In addition to expatriates, many multinational corporations employ third country nationals or non-US expatriates. These employees are citizens of countries other than the United States or of the country in which they are working. An example of a third country national would be a British citizen hired by an American corporation to work in Singapore.

Assignments of less than one year are considered by most companies to be of a temporary nature, and are handled on an expense account or per diem basis.

● *How does one distinguish between those assignments which should be categorized as "globalist" and those as "standard"?*

Generally, the distinction hinges on the duration for which the expatriate is destined to remain overseas and whether he is scheduled for one assignment (standard) or multiple assignments (globalist).

In most cases, "Standard expatriates" are professional or managerial types, housed in developed, urban areas. Conversely, "globalists" will travel anywhere; more often than not, they go to the less desirable, underdeveloped areas where living quarters are not always of their own choosing. They are prepared to move from country to country as and when the company identifies a need for their services.

● *Should "career expatriates" and "short term expatriates" be compensated differently?*

Basically, I think not, although some companies have tried to link career expatriates to the host country rate schedules. The expatriate compensation package ought to be fundamentally the same for both, although peripheral benefits and administrative policies will vary between the two categories of expatriate, and these are addressed later in this booklet.

● *Should policies be conceived to assure, in the case of "career expatriates," a gradual adaptation to the host country?*

If the career expatriate is continually on the move, such a policy would not be feasible. However, in some instances, both standard and globalist expatriates find themselves, either by choice or at the company's request, assigned to one location for a lengthy period of time. As the employee adapts to the culture and economics of the host country, many companies gradually move them toward the host country remuneration system and phase out the expatriate benefits. This measure is intended to lessen the resentment of local nationals who assess the expatriate's worth somewhat below his cost to the operation.

I personally do not believe that *adaptation* is really the issue. If there is a genuine business need that necessitates the use of an expatriate, pay him in full. If that need disappears but he wishes to stay, convert him immediately to the local payroll. Adaptation, to my mind, serves no purpose other than to suggest that management cannot make up its mind whether it needs an expatriate or not.

● *In theory, we are told to pay an expatriate enough to "keep him whole" plus a certain savings element, but in reality, don't we end up paying whatever price he decides is sufficient to make the transfer worthwhile?*

In certain unique situations, for example, where a highly skilled specialist is needed for overseas assignment and he is the only person qualified to handle the task, the cards are very much stacked in his favor. He is in a very strong negotiating position, and, if his expatriation is vitally important to the success of an overseas project, you will probably have to meet his price.

Conversely, if you employ large numbers of expatriates, it could be a source of great discontentment should they discover inconsistencies in the terms of their contracts. Where large numbers of expatriates are employed, consistency of application is vitally important, even if it means a skilled specialist is rejected in favor of somebody less skilled or by a new employee.

● *When expatriates and third country nationals do the same job side-by-side in an overseas location, should they receive equal remuneration?*

This is a difficult question to address, and any answer will be highly subjective, but it is one which is being faced more and more by multinational corporations which not only expatriate Americans, but also expatriate third country nationals from their home bases to other locations (e.g., a Briton to Singapore or a German to France).

The problem is, if you pay expatriates and third country nationals working side-by-side the same rate, you must inherently set your pay scale at the highest common demoninator. This can be not only very costly, but may also be inequitable, since persons expatriating from low base rate countries would receive a tremendous boost in earnings (and standard of living), whereas a person from a high base rate country would receive no significant increase. There would be an incentive disparity which could create even more problems. The solution which works well for most companies necessitates the expatriate package being pegged to a home base rate with the same percentage inducement given to all. Living cost differentials are then calculated to ensure that an expatriate is able to maintain the same standard of living in the country of assignment as he would at home.

Naturally, this does result in different earnings levels for different nationalities who may be performing the same job overseas. While this lends itself to some economies in labor costs, I suspect that in time those third country nationals who perceive themselves as a source of cheap labor may become dissident. Ironically though, when one looks at the world compensation ladder, U.S. earnings levels have gradually fallen behind countries such as Germany, France, Belgium, Holland, and Brazil. Before long, it might be U.S. expatriates who are pleading for equal compensation while on overseas assignment.

● *What is meant by the "international cadre" approach to compensating expatriates?*

This concept has been tested by many companies in an effort to eliminate the differentials in gross income among expatriates who have comparable responsibilities and who work side-by-side but happen to be of different nationalities. In essence, all expatriates receive the equivalent of U.S. salaries and benefits, with cost-of-living differentials pegged at the United States to country of assignment rate instead of at country of origin to country of assignment rates. For reasons discussed in the previous question, I do not think this approach is very workable. It is expensive; it is inequitable in that it offers disproportionate inducements; it hinders recruitment from high-paying countries; and it is generally unmanageable, especially when large numbers of expatriates are involved.

● *What is meant by the "balance sheet approach" to paying expatriates?*

Simply stated, the balance sheet concept is predicated upon the belief that, aside from a premium to be paid for going foreign, an individual should neither gain nor lose, nor have his standard of living materially altered as a result of expatriation.

Given the set of circumstances in a foreign location, there will be items that cost more and items that cost less. By balancing all the components, the net result will be a positive or negative adjustment which, when applied to a base salary, will keep the expatriate economically the same as if he had remained in the United States. This whole approach is discussed at some length in chapter 5.

● *What is the history behind U.S. tax laws as they pertain to expatriates, and what impact did the tax reform act of 1978 have on the cost of doing business abroad?*

In 1926, the Revenue Act provided that a U.S. citizen who was a "bona fide nonresident of the United States for more than six months during a calendar year," could exclude all income earned in foreign countries. Subsequent re-enactments and amendments supported this measure which was aimed at encouraging citizens to go abroad and promote American enterprise.

A 1953 modification to the law required uninterrupted expatriation outside the United States for a period which encompassed a whole taxable year, and extended a $20,000 annual exclusion to taxpayers who were not bona fide foreign residents, but who were physically present in a foreign location(s) for 510 days out of an eighteen-month period. For those bona fide residents who resided abroad for three years or more, the exclusion increased to $25,000. Under these provisions, the expatriate reduced his income by the excluded amount and then claimed a credit or deduction for all taxes paid to foreign governments. Again, this provision was intended to encourage U.S. citizens to go overseas and, in selling American goods, create jobs for Americans back home.

On October 4, 1976, former president Gerald Ford signed the Tax Reform Act of 1976, the provisions of which were to be retroactively effective to January 1, 1976. These provisions reduced the amount of earned income exclusion to $15,000 and prohibited foreign taxes paid on this excluded income from being claimed as either a credit or deduction. Also, taxes were calculated at a rate including the $15,000, then reduced by the amount of the tax on $15,000 calculated as if it were the full taxable income. The result would have been that taxes were calculated at the highest possible rate, then reduced by the tax on $15,000 calculated at the lower rate. Such was the outcry when the true impact of this law became apparent, that the Senate Finance Committee postponed implementation of the Tax Reform Act of 1976.

Since most multinational companies utilize the balance sheet approach, under which a hypothetical tax is withheld from the expatriate regardless of actual taxes incurred, any increases in either U.S. or foreign taxes simply constitute an added cost to the company, a cost which could seriously damage its competitive posture when operating against non-U.S. multinational companies whose governments avoid indirect taxation which might discourage the overseas promotion of their products.

On October 15, 1978, Congress passed the Foreign Earned Income Act of 1978, which resolved much of the controversy resulting from the 1976 Reform Act and ended a two-year period of uncertainty and frustration for expatriates. It was signed by former president Carter on November 6, 1978. As mentioned previously, the Reform Act of 1976 substantially reduced the benefits of the foreign earned income exclusion. The 1978 Act in effect nullified the provisions of the 1976 legislation by delaying the effective date until 1978 and then giving the taxpayer the option to claim a new collection of deductions based on excess foreign living costs. Taxpayers who qualified for the foreign earned income exclusion were given an automatic extention by the Internal Revenue Service until November 15, 1978, to file their 1977 returns.

The foreign earned income provisions effective for years prior to 1976 were made applicable to 1977. Therefore, the exclusion of $20,000 or $25,000 continued through 1977. In this connection, individuals who claim the foreign earned income exclusion and foreign tax credit are required to itemize their deductions.

● *Are we (the United States) the only country that taxes on a basis of nationality rather than residence?*

Australia is the only other country which under certain circumstances (i.e., if the income has not been subject to taxation by another government) will tax nonresident citizens on income earned outside the country.

● *One vice president I know genuinely believes all expatriates are grossly overpaid, live in absolute luxury (drinking "Chevas Regal") and are quite oblivious of the harsh realities of life here in the United States. The expatriates, on the other hand, see themselves as pioneers, risking their health and sanity to promote American products for a modicum of incentive and appreciation. Who's right?*

In actual fact, neither of these renditions of expatriate life is entirely true, although many extremes do exist. I have witnessed "doodlebuggers" working on seismic crews in the Indonesian jungle and in the Libyan desert who really do have a haid time of it; yet, in Rio de Janeiro, I met some nicely tanned expatriates living it up on Cococabana beach. It is really the luck of the draw—Port Harcourt, Nigeria, or the French Riviera—I have worked in both places and for the same incentive premium.

The biggest complaint I hear from expatriates is something along the lines of "nobody in the corporate headquarters understands what it's like out here. If they would only hire somebody in corporate personnel who has served as an expatriate, life would be a lot simpler." Interesting, but not exactly true. Ask yourself, is it necessary for every justice of the peace to have been a criminal before he can fairly administer the law, or for a brain surgeon to have been a recipient of brain surgery? While first hand knowledge in some fields is an advantage, it definitely is not a panacea. Most companies strive to pay their expatriates fairly and administer them equitably, and, given the right resources, there is no reason why this cannot be achieved in an unprejudiced and impartial fashion. If the company's policies are too liberal, don't criticize the expatriates, rewrite the policies to make them competitive with other companies in the same line of business. The same applies to policies which are too austere. There is enough data available today to structure a package that overly favors neither the employee nor the employer at the expense of the other.

● *What part will expatriates play in future growth of multinational companies? Will there be more or fewer expatriates in 1990 than there are today?*

My answer to this two-part question is very speculative, but not inconsistent with trends already beginning to surface around the world. The European Economic Community, for example, has already done much to eliminate national boundaries in Europe. Yesterday's provincial European companies have defined new economic horizons, and today's businessmen roam Europe with a new freedom to sell goods in a multiplicity of markets. Note, however, that these mobile businessmen are not expatriates; they are simply performing the same job, but in a larger arena.

I believe that for multinational firms to survive and grow over the next ten years, they must become international companies instead of companies based on U.S. or European domination of key positions. If today's cost predictions are accurate, expatriates will be too expensive for the firms of 1990; therefore, a company's existence will hinge on its capacity to develop managers and technicians of different nationalities. This means eliminating today's chauvinism at the U.S. or European level by cultivating positive attitudes toward and working effectively with people of other nations. In the short term, we may see a greater deployment of expatriates as firms strive to identify and develop local nationals. However, once these local nationals begin to function as true worldwide executives, having liberated their nationalistic tendencies and hurdled language and cultural barriers, the expatriate will cease to exist as we know him today. As executives of world corporations, they will be viewed as citizens of the world, and therefore, subject to uncompensated expropriation.

Chapter 2

Selection Criteria

If an ass goes travelling, he'll not come home a horse.
—Thomas Fuller

"Abroad" is a big place. It encompasses the entire globe outside the confines of the United States. However, the growth of sophisticated telecommunication techniques and high-speed air transport are gradually making that big place much more accessible. The opportunities for human mobility are increasing, and, judging by the ever-increasing number of expatriates, the urge to work abroad is strong.

Many people are motivated by a sense of adventure, a wish to travel and see a wider world. There are many who have a strong sense of charitableness and who want to help in the economic and social development of third world countries in whatever way they can, and there are those whose relocation is purely vocationally oriented. Whatever the motivation and the destination sought, it takes courage to uproot oneself and one's family and leave familiar surroundings for the unknown.

Expatriation to an extraneous environment where the culture, language, and customs are alien to the average American can be a demanding and exceedingly frustrating experience.

11

It takes a certain type of individual to successfully meet such a challenge, and, because expatriate failures and turnovers are costly, it necessitates great diligence on the part of a personnel director in screening prospective candidates—the man best qualified technically is not always the man who can do the best job abroad! Prospective expatriates have got to be adaptable, independent, and sincere; they must have a real desire to go overseas and the ability to tolerate different behavioral, cultural, social, and religious norms and to learn to empathize with local problems ranging from poverty and disease to political instability and corruption.

Not every expatriate needs these qualities in constant proportions, yet the more of these qualities present in a prospective candidate, the better chance he has of being a successful expatriate. It is equally important, if this candidate is married and has a family, to ensure that the family members also have the desired qualities to make successful expatriates. Many ambitious, career-minded husbands have failed on international assignments because their wives and children were unable to overcome the abrupt changes in language, culture, climate, and living conditions abroad.

Unsuitable human resources cannot be turned into successful expatriates, just as not everybody steeped in the theory of painting can blossom into a Pierre Auguste Renoir or a Vincent van Gogh. It is cruel folly in any walk of life to place a man in a position for which he has none of the inherent skills. Maladjustment is inevitable. An unhappy expatriate who is unable to adjust to the new environment in which you have placed him will slowly become ineffective and a burden to those around him. He will become melancholy and conscious of solitude and isolation, and his home environment will suddenly assume a tremendous importance. Everything American becomes illogically glorified, and all aspects of the foreign location become repugnant—to preserve good labor relations in the overseas subsidiary, you are left with no choice but to repatriate. Whose fault is it that this man did not succeed overseas?

My experience has been that engineering and technical departments often identify candidates for overseas assignments without involving a personnel manager until after a commitment has been made. This is a grave mistake. A personnel manager, more than anyone else, can assess whether the person identified has the qualities that make a good expatriate. As I mentioned earlier, not every expatriate needs a given collection of qualities in constant proportions, but the importance of each one can best be assessed by the one person whose everyday vocation is interacting with people and coordinating their activities. Human beings vary in their abilites, potentialities, and behavior, a fact easily observable but often overlooked by managers with preconceived ideas.

As you will see in chapter 9, utilizing expatriates is exceedingly costly, but since there will always be foreign locations where technical and scientific skills and managerial competence are sadly lacking, we must continue to send them. Recruiting the right man the first time and making sure he is prepared, both vocationally and mentally, for the change in role he is about to experience can have a significant impact on the cost of the international operation.

Always keep in the back of your mind that most people are neophobiacs—they fear and hate anything new or any deviation from their normal life-style.

In summary, here is a selection criteria list:

1. Is the person self-reliant and resourceful with the verve and assiduity to work without direction and supervision? In most cases he will have nobody to turn to in time of crisis or abnormal pressure. Rugged individualism must be a strong point.

2. Does the candidate possess a great deal of tolerance and understanding, especially desirable for underdeveloped countries where language, thought processes, work skills

and general beliefs differ significantly from "the American way?" He needs insight, an intuitive understanding of men and women, and a sensitivity which will enable him to respect local customs and ways of life, while at the same time imparting expertise and knowledge.

3. Leadership by example is a must; will the candidate be able to command the respect of the people with whom he will be working by exhibiting superior knowledge and ability?

4. The candidate must not harbor any prejudices against other races or religions and must display political impartiality.

5. The candidate's family must be adaptable and unprovincial. They must share a willingness to loosen old social ties and move to a different social, cultural and religious environment. The candidate's spouse must be that *beau ideal* who will stick by him no matter what.

6. It should go without saying that any of the following problems should render a candidate ineligible: a history of bad health; alcoholism or drug problems; marital problems; emotional instability; or hang-ups about religion, racism, politics, etc.

Chapter 3

Orientation and Training

There is no road too long to the man who advances deliberately and without haste; there are no honors too distant to the man who prepares himself for them with patience.
—Jean de la Bruyere

ANY DISLOCATION FROM the environment that a person knows well will take its toll, and, since most companies view advance trips to the country of assignment as economically unfeasible, any form of predeparture tutelage or indoctrination becomes very important. If you stop to consider the adjustments necessary for a routine move from one part of the United States to another in terms of different climate, terrain, and regional mannerisms, the intangible adjustments an American must make consciously, subconsciously, and physically to be a good expatriate will seem even more untenable. Predeparture orientations which focus on items that reflect each family's perspective and needs will help equip them for a satisfactory adjustment to the overseas environment. Whether you decide to run an in-house orientation program or use the training facilities provided by independent organizations, remember, the better the employee's preparation for the abrupt changes in foreign language, culture, living conditions, climate, and working environment, the better his chances of success overseas. The more you do to lessen the family's cultural shock, the sooner they will adjust and become good expatriates.

Immediately after an employee has been selected and the terms and conditions of the expatriate assignment agreed upon, it is important that the employee and his family begin immediately learning as much about the country of assignment as possible. Aside from the obvious differences such as language and customs, there are numerous other contrarieties for which the family will be unprepared. They must know something about:

- The geographical location, terrain, climate, history, and culture of the host country.
- The native language and whether English is widely spoken.
- The people who live there and living conditions in general.
- Government and political leanings.
- Legislation (income tax, import/export tariffs, exchange controls, labor laws, etc.) under which he must operate.
- Rates of exchange, currency, and banking arrangements.
- Availability of housing and how it differs from what they are used to.
- Schooling and further education facilities.
- Shopping facilities, goods, and services availability.
- Health care facilities (hospitals, doctors, dentists and pharmacies).
- Social/sports clubs, recreation amenities, and religious activities.
- Automobile availability and cost and alternative methods of ground transportation.
- Appliances and furniture to be shipped and those to be stored.
- What clothing to take.
- The goals and objectives of the assignment.

He must be able to reach an early decision on whether:

- To enroll in a language course.
- To take his children with him or arrange for them to attend private boarding school.
- To ship his furniture or only selected items.
- To pack winter or summer clothing (or both).
- To stock up on certain drugs or medicines.
- To ship or find a home for the family pet.

The personnel director of the specific group selecting the expatriate should be responsible for appropriate orientation and briefing before the individual departs for an overseas location. As a minimum, the employee should be provided with available literature on living and working in the country of assignment. If possible, discussions should be arranged with expatriates who have lived in the country or with employees who, as a result of repeated business visits, are familiar with the environment. Necessary language training and legal and tax counseling must be scheduled before expatriation.

Many companies find themselves expatriating a continual flow of employees to certain countries or to fill certain roles. Why? Not because the local nationals are incompetent, but because the company does not clearly define one of the primary objectives of the expatriate assignment prior to departure. They do not plan for the future. When you send an expatriate anywhere, set him this goal. During orientation, make it clear that one of his objectives is to identify and train a suitable local manager to replace him within a given number of years. Then measure the expatriate by his ability to direct events toward the goal.

Language Training

Most companies will, where necessary, provide language training for the employee and spouse prior to departure and on arrival at the overseas location. Normally the ability to converse is considered sufficient to ease and enrich the stay overseas, but more extensive schooling may be authorized where ability to write in the local language is essential. It is not considered normal practice for companies to pay the cost of language training for children unless extenuating circumstances make it necessary (e.g., as a stipulation for entering a local school). The duration of study will vary among individuals, but generally 120–150 hours should be the maximum required for good conversational ability.

Pre-Assignment Tax Counseling

One of the most important objectives of predeparture orientation is to ensure that the expatriate understands the company's philosophy and policies with regard to personal income tax obligations while on assignment. Most companies make it a condition of expatriate assignment that the employee utilize the services of a designated public accounting firm to prepare both U.S. and work-country returns. Ensuring tax compliance in both the United States and the foreign country of assignment demands expert, up-to-date counsel, but the more the expatriate knows of the problems and alternatives, the better equipped he will be to maintain good records and assist the person designated to prepare and file his returns. Predeparture counseling, with a representative from the designated public accounting firm in attendance, is invaluable and should address as a minimum:

- Record retention
- Return due dates and filing requirements (both U.S. and overseas)
- Taxable compensation
- Earned income exclusion (Tax Reform Act of 1978)
- Foreign tax credits
- Estimated taxes (Form 1040ES)

- Capital gains
- Foreign tax provisions and requirements

The IRS Publication 54 "Tax Guide for U.S. Citizens Abroad" discusses the special problems of U.S. citizens who work overseas and a copy should be given to each expatriate to read and take with him. In addition, the following government tax publications may be useful: Foreign Tax Credit for U.S. Citizens and Resident Aliens (No. 514); Tax Information on Moving Expenses (No. 521); Tax Information on Selling Your Home (No. 523); and Tax Guide for U.S. Citizens Employed in U.S. Possessions (No. 570). While I have deliberately avoided getting into an in-depth discussion on the Internal Revenue Code as it pertains to Americans overseas, the following points should be stressed to prospective expatriates.

- All American citizens, no matter where they are located, have an obligation to the United States Internal Revenue Service and must file yearly returns even if no liability ensues. This obligation is distinct from any obligation imposed by the tax laws of the foreign country.
- While it is incumbent upon all expatriates to comply with the tax laws of both the United States and the host country, they also have a moral obligation to the company—who is providing the benefit of tax protection or equalization—to take whatever measures are legally permissible to minimize the ultimate tax bill. Levying and collecting taxes is big business and complacency on the part of an expatriate can prove very costly to his employer.

**Trips to a Foreign Location in
Advance of Expatriation**

As I stated in the first paragraph of this chapter, it is seldom considered economically feasible for companies to pay for reconnaissance trips to the foreign location prior to expatriation. That is not to say that all companies operate in this manner. My experience suggests that where the expatriate population of any company is very small (say fewer than ten), the company will sometimes reimburse the round trip airfare and related expenses for the expatriate and spouse to survey the location before agreeing to an international assignment. However, I think this is the exception rather than the rule. If the expatriate and the personnel director have done their homework with regard to orientation, there would be very little to gain from the experience.

One exception which might be worthy of special consideration is that when a particular expatriate is the first one to visit a country, he cannot get advice from his predecessors, since no one has been there before. In this case I would recommend an exploratory trip.

In conclusion, I have summarized the contents of this chapter in a checklist, satisfaction of which should ensure that the employee is suitably prepared for the adjustments necessary to be a successful expatriate.

Orientation Checklist

☐ Nature of the job, its responsibilities and objectives.
☐ Compensation—salary, premiums, allowances, benefits and taxes.
☐ Letter of agreement—terms and conditions.
☐ Personnel policies applicable to overseas assignment:
  - Medical requirements
  - Language training
  - Home sale/lease protection
  - Automobile sale protection
  - Shipping/storage of household effects
  - Travel arrangements (itinerary, stopovers, etc.)
  - Work schedules, holidays and vacations
  - Overseas housing

- Schooling and further education
- Tax counseling
- Emergencies
- Repatriation
☐ Documentation
  - Passports, visas, work permits, vaccination certificates
  - Birth certificates, marriage certificate, insurance policies, tax records
☐ Orientation and briefing on living conditions, climate and culture.

Chapter 4

Relocation Policies, Programs, and Allowances

Unless all expatriates share a common doctrine, they will devise their own conflicting policies and divergent procedures. Very soon homogeneity will be lost, costs will escalate and the resultant confusion will arouse the feeling among expatriates that sheer caprice governs policy.

—Stan Frith

ESTABLISHED PRACTICES, procedures, and policies which govern expatriate administration must be set down in writing. This may not seem very appropriate when there are only a small number of expatriates, yet the absence of a policy manual can only lead to indecision and vagueness. A well-conceived, unambiguous reference manual will help to eliminate misunderstandings and friction and help to protect expatriates from errors arising from their own unsupported interpretation of verbal instructions and explanations. Also, where the area of uncertainty and speculation is reduced, fewer will be tempted to a breach of policy in the knowledge that they cannot plead ignorance of practice and procedure.

An expatriate must not be distracted from the principal objectives of his assignment by having to establish his own methods and standards of performance, but should instead benefit from the accumulated experience and knowledge of others. There will be a saving of time; administrative controls will be strengthened; and all personnel matters will be handled uniformly. In summary, the documenting of instructions, policies, and procedures clarifies thought, aids in the prediction of comparable events, and, allied to a sound compensation program, will—

- Attract and retain men who can do the best job overseas.
- Minimize the anxieties and inconvenience associated with relocating people to different environments.
- Cushion the hardships associated with abrupt changes in language, culture, climate, and living and working conditions abroad.
- Ensure administrative uniformity and control.
- Eliminate financial uncertainties by providing a compensation package that is sustainable.

Unlike domestic relocations, where long-standing policies are seldom if ever updated, international relocation policies should be continually subject to reappraisal and review. Policies that suit one industry group may not necessarily be consistent with the needs of another. Where some companies are extremely liberal and seem hesitant to make changes for fear of damaging morale and losing key expatriates, others which find themselves under increasing pressures to control escalating expatriate costs, continually but cautiously experiment with policies.

Because of worldwide inflation and other international economic developments, companies must continually monitor the philosophy, purpose, and application of the compensation package. Similarly, the administration and impact of noncompensation policies must be periodically tested and, where necessary, updated. This assumes, of course, that policies already exist. If they do not and you are about to begin drafting your first expatriate procedures manual, I am of the opinion that the following areas must be addressed as a minimum.

Documentation

Before leaving the United States, every expatriate must have a valid passport. This proof of American citizenship can be issued either to individuals or to families, but I suggest that you insist on separate passports for each family member. This will eliminate any problems should they wish to travel separately. Appendix I at the end of chapter 11 provides complete information for passport applicants, plus a sample of Department of State form DSP II.

The United States government is stringent with visa and work permit regulations for foreigners, and so are most foreign governments. Requirements vary from country to country, as does the time taken to process them. Be sure that nobody leaves for an assignment without the correct visas and permits —this can be facilitated by submitting the necessary applications to the foreign consulate or visa office as soon as the employee accepts the terms and conditions of the overseas assignment.

Any costs associated with obtaining visas, work permits, or passports should be reimbursed by the company.

Assignment Letter

Most companies insist that an expatriate sign an international service agreement letter prior to departure, outlining the terms, conditions, and duration of the expatriate assignment. An example of a typical assignment letter is illustrated in chapter 7.

Medical Examinations and Immunizations

Before an employee is accepted for an international assignment, the employee and accompanying dependents must undergo a thorough medical examination to ensure that they are fit for life abroad. Similarly, visits to a dentist and an optician should be scheduled well ahead of time, thereby allowing time for any treatment prior to relocation.

The company physician or a designated doctor should specify the types of immunization required for the area of international assignment. Any expenses incurred by the expatriate in getting the prescribed medical treatment and immunizations should be reimbursed by the company.

Household Effects—Shipment or Storage?

Shipment of an expatriate's household effects to the overseas location can be a costly aspect of relocation. As a result, many companies try to control this expense by defining the overall maximum weight for which they are prepared to pay. In many instances, the availability of furnished accommodation, or the ability to rent furniture in the work location will dictate which is the best route. It is useful to note, however, that even in places where furnished accommodation is available, there is a break-even point where the overseas cost of leasing furniture plus domestic storage costs will exceed cost of shipping. Generally, I believe that if the assignment is for two years or less, it is more economical to provide furnished accommodation overseas and ship only personal effects. On assignments in excess of two years, provided the family is not continually moving, it may be economically advantageous for the company and more desirable for the expatriate family to have their own furniture shipped to the overseas location. When this is the case, most companies will arrange and make payment for the surface freight shipment of household goods and effects to include packing and crating, insurance, demurrage, transportation, customs clearance, import duties, delivery, and unpacking. Restrictions would normally prohibit the shipment of bulky or high value items such as automobiles, boats, trailers, motorcycles, heavy machinery, pianos, antiques, jewelry, furs, etc. Any employee who wished to ship such items could still do so, but at his own expense.

Recent surveys indicate there is a wide range of policies regarding the shipment of household effects. Since the objective of this book is not to list a variety of alternatives but to propose specific policies, the following would represent a fairly competitive posture.

2-3 Year Assignment	Single	Married	Per Child
Surface	4,000 lbs.	7,500 lbs.	1,000 lbs.
Air	500 lbs.	1,000 lbs.	250 lbs.
3-5 Year Assignment			
Surface	5,000 lbs.	10,000 lbs.	1,500 lbs.
Air	500 lbs.	1,000 lbs.	250 lbs.

The company would store the remainder of an employee's household goods for the duration of the assignment. For distant assignments (e.g., Australia, Japan, or locations in Asia), most companies make a more concerted effort to discourage the shipment of household goods. Instead, they make available company-owned furniture.

Normally, companies will not ship automobiles to foreign locations unless extenuating circumstances make it economical or practical to do so. American-made autos tend to be impractical and uneconomical anywhere outside of the United States. The unavailability of spare parts, excessive shipping costs, customs restrictions, import duties, and high gasoline prices intimate that selling one's car(s) prior to departure is the most desirable procedure. Where this is the policy, companies usually protect the employee in the sale of up to two autos prior to departure. Reimbursement for the difference, if any, between selling price and fair market value as listed in the N.A.D.A. official used car guide is considered reasonable and customary.

Should an employee dispose of his vehicle a week or so prior to departure, reimbursement for the rental of an automobile for the interim period up to actual date of departure is normal practice.

Real Estate Assistance (Sale or Lease Protection)

Real estate assistance is offered by a majority of companies, because they recognize that the disposal of a home is probably the single most important obstacle facing an employee relocating overseas. It is not only a very costly aspect of relocation, but, if not taken care of properly, it can become a source of constant distraction for the employee on international assignment. Generally, there are two options open to the employee—to sell, or to lease his residence—and these are addressed below.

HOME SALE PROTECTION

When an employee elects to sell his house as a result of an international transfer, most companies offer assistance with the sale or reimbursement of selling expenses. Assistance is normally limited to the sale of the employee's primary place of residence and not to income-generating property, summer homes, etc. Expenses eligible for reimbursement would include brokerage fees, appraisal costs, attorneys' fees, recording and satisfaction of mortgage, federal tax stamps, transfer taxes, title insurance, loan discount points, and any other costs normally paid by the seller, provided the sale is made through a legally licensed real estate broker. In addition, many companies will protect the employee against forced-sale losses by ensuring he receives the present fair market value. This is accomplished by obtaining two or three appraisals from independent real estate appraisers, averaging them, and compensating the employee for the difference, if any, between the averaged fair market value and the actual selling price.

LEASE PROTECTION

Many companies provide the employee with the option of leasing his home while on assignment as an alternative to selling it, thereby protecting his investment from possible loss due to inflation or higher mortgage interest rates.

An ideal method of operating lease protection is as follows. If the allowable expenses incurred in maintaining and leasing the residence, on a cumulative basis, exceed income from the property, the company should reimburse the difference up to the amount of a hypothetical broker's selling commission or some other specified amount. Allowable expenses under most lease protection programs include mortgage payments (principal, interest, taxes, and insurance), utility bills, real estate management fees, yard and pool maintenance, cleaning, advertising for tenants, and minor repairs. Any net deficit reimbursed by the company in one fiscal quarter would be offset against future profits and vice versa, the objective being that the expatriate neither gains nor loses from the rental transaction, yet does benefit from appreciation on the value of his or her property. Leaving the house vacant is, to my mind, not a viable alternative for obvious reasons.

Resettlement Allowance

An expatriate incurs many unpredictable, out-of-pocket expenses when transferred overseas. These may occur in the United States prior to departure, or when the expatriate arrives in the overseas location. They include—

- Charges for connection or disconnection of utilities
- Cleaning services (carpets, drapes, etc.)
- Adapting and modifying household appliances to different voltages and frequencies, purchase of transformers, plugs, light fixtures, etc.
- Automobile licensing, registration, and tax
- Loss of plants, food supplies, and liquor

A recent survey I conducted indicates that most companies simply reimburse actual out-of-pocket expenses incurred by employees while relocating overseas. I see no problem with this, except that it is sometimes difficult to assess the value of food, liquor, or plants which are given away prior to departure. Another alternative to compensate for these incidental expenses, and one widely used by companies to meet specific needs on the basis of expediency, is to grant the expatriate a lump sum allowance based on salary. The following is a typical example of how it might be structured:

	Departing U.S. Salary	Returning to U.S. Salary
Married or single homeowner (actually living in owned house)	1½ months	1 month
Married lessee	1 month	1 month
Single lessee	½ month	½ month

The above example assumes that in the overseas location all expatriates occupy leased accommodation or are housed in company-provided housing.

Temporary Living Expenses

In the event an employee finds it necessary to vacate his present living quarters prior to the date of departure, or should the employee not be able to find or move directly into regular housing on arrival in the overseas location, companies normally reimburse hotel expenses or pay a per diem for periods up to three weeks or (in some cases) for as long as the expatriate is in transient status. A policy of this nature would provide the expatriate with adequate time to locate housing in the foreign location; this is especially important where pre-assignment house-hunting trips are not permitted. It would also eliminate many of the problems which would otherwise face an expatriate while awaiting the arrival of household goods and personal effects.

Clothing Allowance

Although not a common practice, some companies assist an expatriate with the cost of equipping his family with suitable clothing for the overseas place of work. Not only is this allowance helpful when an expatriate from Florida finds himself working in Scandinavia, but it is also useful to the expatriate who, because of different routines and customs in the work country, finds that a new wardrobe is a consequence of his expatriation.

What is construed as an equitable amount varies considerably from country to country. Obviously, fur coats and lined boots will be more expensive than tropical shirts and bermuda shorts. Since I have no statistics to quote from, all I can suggest is that you review each situation on a case-by-case basis, or seek the advice of one of the consultants listed in chapter 12, who I believe have conducted some surveys in which this subject was addressed.

Travel

With very few exceptions, companies will pay direct route, economy class, jet air transportation for the employee, spouse, and dependent (unmarried) children. If the employee and his family wish to travel by any other means (surface transportation or combination air and surface) and if time is not of the essence, most companies will reimburse up to the cost of direct routing by economy jet air travel. Some companies will pay first class travel or reimburse stopover expenses for trips over a certain number of hours (say eight to twelve or more hours). I think this a sound practice, especially if small children are accompanying the expatriate. Incidentally, while talking about small children, although infants can travel free if seated on the parents' lap, I recommend the company purchase a seat. This will make the journey a lot easier for the family, and the seat carries with it an additional baggage allowance which could cut back on some air freight costs.

The majority of multinational companies assume responsibility for making all reservations and delivering the tickets to the expatriate. He will have enough to worry about without chasing down air tickets. Furthermore, expenses that are incident to relocation travel, such as passports, visas, health certificates, taxis, airport buses, gratuities, excess baggage charges, airport taxes, and required lodging and meals en route, should be reimbursed.

If a company-sponsored travel insurance program is not offered, I suggest you reimburse the expatriate for the cost of acquiring his own. The time he could waste in terms of pursuing lost personal possessions and damaged or lost baggage could well exceed the cost of insurance.

Chapter 5

The Compensation Package

*In good conscience, every expatriate should first examine
the possibility that his real problem is not the high cost of
living so much as the cost of high living.*

—Stan Frith

THE HEART OF ADMINISTERING any expatriate program is the
formalization of policies and procedures for paying the expatriate in a satisfactory and competitive manner. The criteria
of what is satisfactory has changed dramatically in the last
few years as inflation and gyrating exchange rates have complicated the one area of expatriate administration that for
decades had remained stable and relatively predictable.

Beginning in the 1972–1973 time period, inflation rates
became double digit, not only in the United States, but also
in the principal expatriate work countries of Europe and South
America. The 700 percent plus inflation rate in Argentina is
now folklore in the expatriate compensation community. Consultants whose business it was to provide valid cost of living
indices were finding it increasingly difficult to react, measure,
and publish worldwide cost data before their efforts became

33

redundant due to rampaging increases in the cost of goods and services around the world. Consequently, expatriates became concerned by the rapidly rising costs while still on a fixed income. They became vocal and wanted to understand why they weren't receiving substantially more money. While administrators were trying to address this issue, many currencies began to "float," thus proliferating the problem further in that currencies were constantly changing in their value relative to each other. Expatriates became alarmed to find the value of their compensation package varied from day to day.

Is there a right way of compensating employees assigned overseas? The answer, of course, is yes. There are many right ways. What is good for a company with only ten expatriates may not be right for another company with several hundred. A tailor-made program that comprehends the individual needs of ten expatriates may be totally inappropriate as the number of expatriates grows. Later in this chapter we will examine in some detail the most widely accepted approach to expatriate compensation. It is termed the "balance sheet" approach, and it is used either implicitly or explicitly by most large U.S. multinational corporations. Simply stated, the balance sheet concept is predicated upon the belief that aside from a premium to be paid to the employee for going international, an individual should neither gain nor lose from taking the assignment.

The most salient attributes of the balance sheet concept and the reasons why I personally prefer this approach are as follows:

● The concept works well in a complex and ever-changing environment.
● If administered correctly, it favors neither the employee nor the employer at the expense of the other.
● It ensures that the expatriate is provided with the same

home-country purchasing power regardless of job level, family size, or country of assignment. It keeps the expatriate "whole," and experience has taught me that policies which gravitate toward this objective are judged by employees to be logical, equitable, and sustainable.

● It is reasonably easy to explain and document.
● It is easily updated in line with inflation and exchange rate perturbations.

Keep in mind that your expatriates will know little about the adequacy of the compensation package prior to arriving in the foreign location. Your integrity in designing the compensation program will determine how much confidence and trust the expatriate places in your ongoing efforts to maintain a fair and equitable package. A less than satisfactory job of administering the program will result in your being inundated with a large volume of empirical evidence to substantiate claims for more equitable treatment. It needs little exposition to see that the disruptive effects of this preoccupation would soon begin to reflect in the profits of the overseas subsidiary. At worst, the expatriate may just pack his bags and return home, leaving you not only with a serious staffing problem, but with incurred costs far in excess of the amount you would have saved from penny-pinching on the compensation package.

Many companies make the egregious mistake of developing programs or techniques that are so complex or refined that they become difficult to explain. There is a great temptation to develop policies and procedures which appear to be a panacea for a given problem, but which are viewed by the expatriates as neither rational nor satisfactory, simply because they cannot understand them.

I believe that if the program is capable of achieving the following objectives, you will avoid most of the problems that might otherwise result. The program should:

- Ensure that an expatriate neither gains nor loses as a result of differences in the cost of living, currency fluctuations, and additional taxes encountered while working abroad.
- Be competitive with the compensation policies employed by other multinational industries.
- Maintain a reasonable and equitable relationship to domestic compensation programs and personnel policies.
- Further the company's ability to freely transfer expatriates between international locations.

The "Balance Sheet" Approach—An Overview

The following brief summary addresses the components of the balance sheet concept, which I believe satisfy the objectives outlined above while still retaining sufficient flexibility to meet the unique requirements of individual companies. What I shall attempt to do at this juncture is simply to acquaint you with the terms and objectives and then get into the details of each component later on in the chapter.

BASE SALARY

While abroad, an expatriate should receive the same base salary as he would for a comparable position in the domestic operation. No matter what other considerations are factored into his package, the base salary component should be kept clean, thereby enabling both the company and the employee to retain visibility of his relative position in the home country rate range. This is very important, especially at the time of repatriation when the returning employee must be reintegrated into the domestic salary structure.

INTERNATIONAL SERVICE PREMIUM

This represents the real incentive for the employee to relocate overseas. Usually pegged at a percentage of base salary, this tax-free premium constitutes the only true inducement built into the package, since all the other components are aimed at keeping him whole.

HARDSHIP PREMIUM

Certain jobs require expatriation to undesirable, underdeveloped, or hazardous locations. In recognition of the adverse and onerous conditions under which an expatriate (and possibly his or her family) is being required to live and work, a special premium is paid.

HYPOTHETICAL TAX

It is important that you safeguard an expatriate from any increased tax burdens that might be suffered as a result of: (1) his increased taxable earnings which have been inflated by premiums and allowances; (2) the fact that many foreign countries tax individuals at a higher rate than does the United States; and (3) his being subject, in some instances, to both U.S. and foreign income taxes. It should also be noted that hypothetical tax also prevents windfall situations when the work-country taxes plus the home-country taxes are less than what he would have paid at home.

Suffice it to say at this point that the term hypothetical tax refers to the tax the expatriate would normally pay had he not accepted an expatriate assignment. This estimate is limited to federal tax liabilities and does not comprehend the various state and local taxes. In addition, it should be noted that the estimate is based on the employee's company-source income; his total income tax may actually be more depending on the magnitude of his outside income.

LIVING COST DIFFERENTIAL

This item is an allowance intended to provide the expatriate with the amount of local currency necessary to keep him "whole;" that is, to ensure that he neither gains nor loses in his effort to maintain a comparable standard of living in the country of assignment. The allowance should be computed such that, economically, the expatriate will be the same as if he had remained at home in terms of purchasing power. There are two components to the living cost differential (LCD): first, there is a housing differential to comprehend the additional housing cost; and second, there is a differential to provide for the additional costs of purchasing a market basket of goods and services.

POSITION ALLOWANCE

In rare instances it is conceivable that the sum of base salary plus LCD, less hypothetical tax, could still result in an expatriate earnings level that is lower than for a peer employee in the work country, and this could be potentially embarrassing to the expatriate. The phenomenon is especially prevalent when dealing with third country nationals who are expatriated from a low base rate country to a high base rate country. Many companies ensure this does not happen by calculating a "position allowance," which will boost the expatriate's earnings to a level that as a minimum is equal to his work-country peers.

SALARY SPLIT

It is a generally accepted practice that expatriates will be paid both in the work-country and in the home-country. The amount of base salary normally expended for housing and goods and services plus any living cost differentials is generally paid in the work-country. As a general rule, this amounts to approximately two-thirds of the total package.

The above are only brief descriptions; my intent at this stage is to establish what it takes to keep an expatriate "whole." One other important aspect is to look for a way of displaying the various components which serves as a good record for personnel purposes, while at the same time providing a clear and concise breakdown of the compensation package for the expatriate.

Fig. 5.1. Expatriate Compensation Package
(Personal and Confidential)

Employee Data

	Employee	Effective
Name _____	Number _____	Date _____

Assignment Work Location _____

Normal Work Location _____

Work Assignment _____ Job Grade _____

	No. Children	Total No.
Marital Status _____	with Expatriate _____	Tax Dependents ____

Compensation Summary

		Annual Compensation
1.	Base Salary $_____ Per Month	$_____
2.	International Service Premium	$_____
3.	Hardship Premium	$_____
4.	Hypothetical Tax	($_____)
5.	Living Cost Differential	$_____
6.	Position Allowance	$_____
7.	Net Compensation	$_____

Payroll Split

	Per Month	*Per Annum*
Home Country Pay	$_____	$_____
Work Country Pay	$_____	$_____
Exchange Rate: $1 = _____	_____	_____

Figure 5.1 is a suggested format which I have found to be useful in communicating compensation data to expatriates. However, the format is not as important as the information, though, if designed correctly, the format ensures that misun-

derstanding will be held to a minimum. This is no small point, considering the complexity of the subject matter and the questions which invariably surface once the employee reaches the work country. The form should be explicit enough to state the basic situation (family size, country of assignment, etc.), and the relative value that each of the package components yields to the employee, but it should not be needlessly complicated by detailed computations which are better kept on a filed worksheet in the expatriate administrator's office. You will also notice that the form is not intended to cover all indirect compensation items such as educational allowances, provisions for language training, etc., since these items can usually be administered through approved expense statements in a much more efficient manner.

Compensation programs designed for employees working overseas cannot serve the exact same objectives as those designed for domestic use. While an expatriate will establish income disbursement patterns to satisfy his hierarchy of needs, much as he would at home, different economic conditions prevailing abroad can subject an expatriate to financial hardships instead of rewarding him for operating in an extraneous environment under unfamiliar laws and customs. The balance sheet approach is designed to ensure that an expatriate is able to maintain the same standard of living abroad that he had at home, neither gaining nor losing as a result of differences in the cost of living, exchange rates, inflation, or taxation abroad. To comprehend and implement such a system, a personnel administrator has to understand income distribution and spending habits here in the United States—how much people normally allocate to housing, utilities, savings, taxation, food, clothing, etc.—before he can attempt to provide the expatriate with the same purchasing power and living standard abroad. In addition, he has to establish a method for determining or measuring current living conditions and costs, both at home and abroad.

In expatriate compensation, as in other fields, there is diversity of opinion as to what is best for the employee and, to no lesser extent, what is best for the company. Experience has taught me that even today, approaches to expatriate compensation vary from very simple to very complex. Initially, most people will probably consider that the balance sheet concept falls into the latter category. But, I recommend this approach if it is at all possible, and it generally is possible once a corporation decides to commit sufficient resources and dedication to making it happen. This is not to say that the most simple of schemes—say base salary plus a 25 percent share of the profits—does not have its place in the expatriate world today. However, I think these situations are the exception rather than the rule.

The Balance Sheet Approach— A Detailed Analysis

The following detailed analysis and discussion address a specific approach, the balance sheet approach. While many consultant organizations are actively researching and developing innovative approaches in the field of compensation, the following is a concise summary of the state of the art at this time, and it will enable you to use this book as a blueprint for implementing, understanding, and explaining the concept.

COMPONENT 1: BASE SALARY

The importance of base salary is manifest not only in that it enables us to maintain a given standard of living, but, for the expatriate, in that it is also the basis by which the majority of allowances and premiums are determined. Most employee salaries are a function of the place the job occupies within the compensation system of the company and the job market environment as determined by supply and demand. For this reason, great care should be taken to maintain the same basic salary structure for expatriates on international assignment as for peers back home. It is important that an expatriate be paid the same base salary that the company would pay for a comparable job in the United States and that it be reviewed at the same intervals. Failure to maintain this parity will distort the relationship to other jobs within the company (both domestic and international) and make it difficult to reintegrate an expatriate back into the U.S. salary structure on completion of an assignment.

Notwithstanding the above, successful application of the balance sheet approach "requires" that base salaries of expatriates be maintained on a par with their domestic counterparts. Also, an understanding of what base salary means to the domestic employee in terms of satisfying needs must also be acquired before one can structure a program to help satisfy those same needs, but in a foreign environment.

Figure 5.2 is a simple diagram which illustrates what a base salary earned in the United States means in terms of satisfying the domestic needs of the American wage earner. Note that the compartments on the righthand blocks will vary in size depending on income and family size.

An employee's domestic monthly disbursements can be broken down into four general categories; the major three being the cost of housing, the cost of goods and services, and taxes (state, federal, and social security). The other, of course, is savings. It seems logical at this point to establish the principle that these components of cash outflow will be uniquely different for each individual employee and this fact must be comprehended by any program that is developed. For that reason, statistics are now available from various consultants which indicate disbursement patterns or trends for given income levels. You can be assured that the employee is sensitive to his normal domestic cash outflow pattern and will be quick to alert you if, for example, his housing costs have become disproportionate overseas. As you have probably al-

Figure 5.2

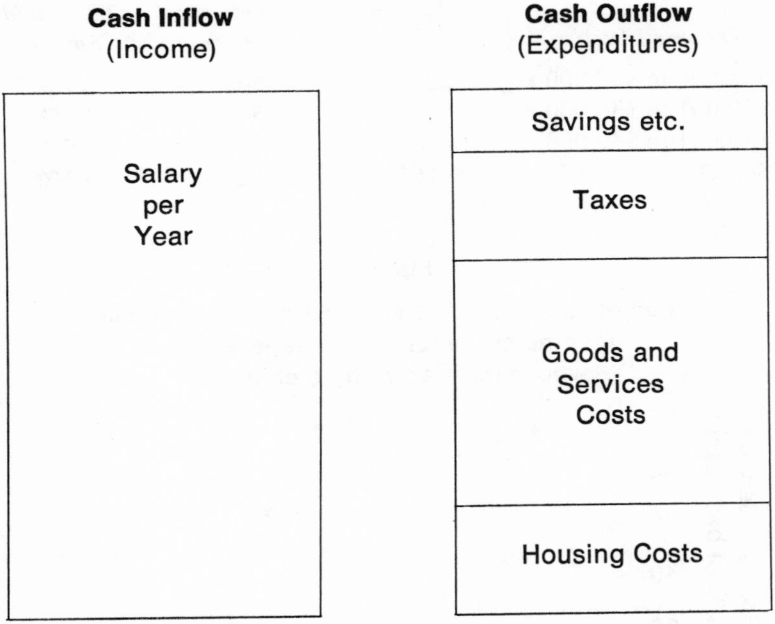

Cash Inflow (Income)	**Cash Outflow** (Expenditures)

ready realized, the statistical distribution varies somewhat depending upon the gross income level. As one's income increases, less and less of the income is spent on goods and services, the excess going to taxes, savings, or investments. Before we depart from this train of thought let's first establish in our minds roughly what a married employee spends for housing and goods and services in the United States, and how the excess does in fact increase. Note that in the following table I have bracketed income levels for convenience. In reality these spending patterns would form a curve on a graph and would vary for every $1000 earned.

Please note that published statistics typically relate to a married employee and do not include the incremental cost

	Percentage of Gross Salary		
Income Level	Housing Costs	Goods and Services	Taxes and Savings
$15,000 to $20,000	25%	54%	21%
$20,001 to $30,000	21%	50%	29%
$30,001 to $40,000	18%	47%	35%
$40,001 to $60,000	16%	42%	42%

Fig. 5.3

As an example, Fig. 5.3 shows a typical spendable income curve for a U.S. wage earner who is married with no children.

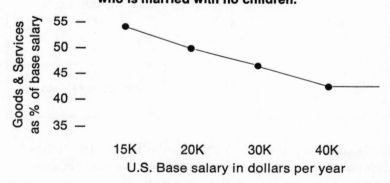

impact of children (or the lower cost of being single). Various adjustments must be made to the above percentages based on the size of the family. The following are surveyed national averages at the time of going to print, and while typical of the population as a whole, are obviously not absolute for any given family. This is to be expected when, for example, you consider that the children of some employees are in college, while others may not yet be in school. Nevertheless, I feel these national averages are adequate for estimating the incremental cost impact of children.

Family Size	Percentage of Married Employee's Living Costs*
Single	85%
Married	100%
Married, one child	107%
Married, two children	113%
Married, three children	118%
Married, four children	123%

*Any cost of living or housing differential calculated on the basis of a married person with no children (which all State Department indices are) should be multiplied by one of these factors.

For example, if an employee makes $30,000 per year, my table estimates that a husband and spouse spend approximately 50 percent of the income on goods and services. If we assume he is not only married, but has two children, then that percentage, factored by 113 percent, equals $16,950 ($30,000 x .50 x 1.13), or 56.5 percent spent yearly on goods and services.

The reason we are discussing these various statistics is because they are key to implementing a balance sheet approach. Before we can achieve our goal of keeping the expatriate "whole," we must first define, at least statistically, what the word whole means from an economic standpoint. For instance, looking at the above example, we have determined that this employee will normally spend about 56.5 percent of his gross income on goods and services in his home country. We can now collect cost data that will help us maintain that same buying power in the work country where goods and services probably cost a great deal more. However, before we proceed further, let's give these statistics a name. The most common term for what we have just covered is *spendable income factor*. What we have looked at so far are factors which are appropriate for the United States. Of course, all countries have unique spendable income patterns, and I recommend they be employed if you find yourself administering non-U.S. expatriates.

What elements or appurtenances are embodied in housing costs and goods and services costs? This question invariably comes up when explanations and presentations are given to expatriates. They want to know if you have made allowances for the fact they must drink bottled water and employ maids and security guards. Do the housing cost percentages include fuel bills? Below is a summary of those items which are generally included in cost indices and spendable income factors:

Goods and Services	*Housing*
Food	Rent or lease cost
Clothing	Utility costs
Gasoline, car maintenance	Required, fixed-cost property
Transportation (this excludes	maintenance fees
the purchase of a car)	
Auto insurance	
Medical care	
Personal care items	
Household equipment	
Domestic help	
Recreation	
Food away from home	
(Generally, anything which	
is consumable. Does not	
include major cost items	
such as cars, boats, land,	
buildings, etc.)	

I have attempted in this base-salary section to introduce you to the statistics which are a major part of understanding expatriate compensation. They form the basis for applying the techniques that I will describe in subsequent parts of this chapter. The key points to remember at this time are:

● Base salary is the most important component of the expatriate's package, and the job evaluation/base pay relationships should be maintained in such a manner that, when the employee returns to the U.S., he will have a base rate comparable to his peers.

● An employee's base salary should always be separately identified on the letter of agreement and should be reviewed periodically in line with domestic policies.

● Employee income can be translated into unique *spendable income* patterns. These statistics define what the word "whole" means to the expatriate administrator.

COMPONENT 2: INTERNATIONAL SERVICE PREMIUM

Under the balance sheet approach, an international service premium represents the one real incentive for the employee to relocate overseas, since all other provisions are aimed at keeping him whole. The premium is usually pegged at a percentage of base salary and is almost universally administered as a tax-free income via the tax equalization calculations. Most companies realize that, inherent in foreign service, there are a considerable number of detractors for which they must offer some form of tangible recognition. These detractors include:

1. Isolation from family and friends and loosening old social ties
2. Unusually difficult working conditions (unfamiliar laws, customs, thought processes, etc.)
3. Different attitudes, values, and perceptions
4. Language and cultural barriers
5. Quality of housing and utilities
6. Changes in educational, religious, and recreational norms

7. Changes in social protocol
8. Climatic adjustments
9. Environmental hostilities, adversities, and complexities
10. Personal safety/exposure (kidnappings, hijacking, etc.)
11. Inferior medical, dental, and health facilities
12. Political differences resulting in lack of freedom to conduct one's life in the fashion to which one is accustomed
13. Possible loss of equity appreciation on U.S. residence

There are a variety of schemes which have been developed for determining the magnitude or percentage of base salary which should be provided as an inducement to the expatriate: it is very difficult to translate or reduce the factors outlined above into one right premium percentage. Notwithstanding this, my experience is that a tax free premium which is 15 percent of base salary provides an adequate and competitive premium. In fact, it is equivalent to a 25 percent before-tax payment for a person in a 40 percent tax bracket.

COMPONENT 3: HARDSHIP PREMIUMS

Certain jobs require expatriation to undesirable, undeveloped, or hazardous locations. In recognition of the adverse and onerous conditions under which some expatriates are required to live and work, a special premium is paid in addition to the regular international service premium. This premium tends to equalize what may otherwise be considered a good or bad assignment location. Premiums are generally expressed as a percent of base salary and vary from country to country depending upon the degree of hardship. Almost without exception, companies compute this premium using data published by the U.S. State Department. The State Department conducts extensive and very detailed surveys and analyses each year to determine what hardship premiums, if any, are justified. Below is an example of some hardship premiums now being advocated:

Country	City	Percent of base salary
Indonesia	Jakarta	15
	other	20-25
Egypt	Alexandria	10
	Cairo	15
Nigeria	Lagos	25
	other	20-25
Korea	Seoul	0
	other	10-15
Lebanon	Beirut	25
	other	10

While these premiums may be perceived as purely a cash bonus, my experience suggests that expatriates in real hardship zones tend to spend more on vacation trips, clothing, medical supplies, and other extras to help offset the unpleasantries; these are expenses which expatriates on regular assignments would not incur, or would incur to a lesser degree.

COMPONENT 4: HYPOTHETICAL TAX (TAX EQUALIZATION)

Possibly no other area of expatriate administration will prove as challenging to you as the myriad of problems and situations inherent in the expatriate tax environment. Indeed, the complexity of tax laws in the home country alone frequently requires the help of professional tax counsel. Your expatriates will not only be subject to the tax laws of the host country, but they will also be subject to a different set of tax laws in the United States. For this reason, policies have been developed to assure the employee that his tax liability will not exceed his normal home-country tax level.

Foremost among the techniques which have been developed to minimize adverse international tax burdens for expatriates is an approach called "tax equalization." The basic premise behind this term is that the company will make the necessary tax payment either directly to the government or through the employee for any amount in excess of what the expatriate would have paid had he remained in the United States. These payments or reimbursements, when added to the employee's "equalized" tax liability, satisfy all taxes of both the home and work country.

Summary of Tax Laws Affecting U.S. Expatriates

All citizens of the United States are subject to federal income taxes regardless of where they reside and are taxed on total income earned and unearned whether paid in the United States or in the work country.

As a result of the Foreign Earned Income Act of 1978, the $20,000 Section 911 exclusion has now been restricted to income earned by individuals residing in certain "camps" located in designated hardship areas. Expatriates who do not live in "camps" are, under Section 913, allowed to deduct certain expenses for living abroad; these could include cost of living differential, excess housing expense, school expenses, home leave travel expenses, and a hardship area deduction of up to $5,000 annually. The eligibility criteria which determines whether an exclusion is warranted or whether the expenses of living abroad may be deducted are twofold. The expatriate must meet one of two tests. The first test is commonly known as the bona fide *residence rule*. To qualify under this rule, the following conditions must be met:

1. The employee must be a bona fide resident of a foreign country (or countries) for an uninterrupted period encompassing an entire tax year. The term "entire tax year" means a full twelve-month period (even for a decedent) and a calendar year for a calendar-year taxpayer. The individual can return to the United States for brief and temporary trips, but he must show a clear

intention of departing from the United States without an unreasonable delay.

2. The taxpayer must have received earned income from qualified foreign sources during the period of uninterrupted bona fide residence.

Qualifying under the above criterion has proved to be a somewhat difficult task, as the individual is generally required to demonstrate his "intent" of remaining in the work country for an extensive period of time. The tax authorities typically examine:

1. the nature of the accommodation held overseas;
2. whether the taxpayer's family reside with him during the year;
3. the total length of time the taxpayer has resided overseas without interruption;
4. the nature and duration of the taxpayer's visa in the overseas country;
5. the assignment period conditions imposed by the employer;
6. whether accommodation is retained by the employee in the United States and, if so, the rental situation and the relationship of any tenants to the taxpayer's family.

It is questions like these—most of which are listed in Part 1 of form 2555—that assist the IRS in determining whether the employee qualifies under this provision of the tax law.

The second and most commonly utilized test is the *physical presence test* which grants the camp exclusion or deductions for expenses of living abroad to U.S. citizens who do not qualify under the bona fide residence test, but who satisfy the following conditions:

1. The individual must be present in a foreign country (or countries) for a total of at least 510 full days during any period of eighteen consecutive months.
2. The taxpayer must have received earned income for the

performance of personal services, and the earned income must be received from qualified foreign sources during the eighteen-month period.

Items Which Are Taxable under U.S. Tax Laws

The tax laws of the United States are rather far reaching with regard to items deemed as taxable income to U.S. expatriates. A quick scan of the following list will give you an insight as to the assortment of items on which tax will be assessed, and it is important that both you and your expatriates know which items must be reported to avoid an embarrassing encounter with the Internal Revenue Service.

This list is a summary of common items which, in addition to direct earnings, must be reported and are taxable. However, a corresponding deduction may also be allowed in some instances:

1. *All tax reimbursements.* Any taxes assessed against the employees which are paid in full or in part by the company, either through reimbursement or directly to taxing authorities on behalf of the employee.

2. *Vacation travel.* Transportation costs for the employee and eligible dependents and any other expenses paid by the company during the vacation period. These costs are generally incurred during home leave.

3. *Education travel.* Travel costs paid by the company for children of the expatriate attending schools away from the employee's point of assignment.

4. *Education assistance.* Tuition and expenses paid by the company to assist the employee in meeting additional educational costs incurred for dependent children as the result of assignment.

5. *Cost of living differentials.* Differentials paid to the expatriate to offset the additional living costs associated with living overseas.

6. *Subsidized housing or automobile costs.* The employee must report the fair market value of housing and/or automobiles furnished by the company. Automobiles are excluded to the extent they are used for business purposes.
7. *Storage charges.* Costs incurred or reimbursed by the company to store the employee's household goods and personal effects while stationed overseas.
8. *International service and hardship premiums.* All premiums paid to the employee associated with working overseas.
9. *Moving expenses.* Relocation expenses incurred by the company in moving the employee and his dependents to and from the work country and within the work country. All relocation expenses should be reported on a gross basis. Employees should apply such exclusions as are allowed by the IRS.
10. *Pre-move travel, meals, and lodging.* Company-paid or reimbursed expenses (motel, car rental, etc.) preceding actual relocation to and from the point of assignment.
11. *Temporary living expenses prior to moving into permanent quarters.* Reimbursement for meals and lodging while occupying temporary accommodation in the overseas location prior to moving into permanent quarters.
12. *Home sale, purchase, or lease protection.* Company-paid expenses in connection with the sale or lease of the employee's former residence. Also, expenses incurred for the purchase of a new residence upon returning to the home country.
13. *Settling-in Expenses.* Any kind of allowance or reimbursement made by the company to defray the costs associated with installation of appliances and other settling-in expenses.

Deductions for Expenses of Living Abroad*

Under Section 913 of the Foreign Earned Income Act, 1978, U.S. citizens who satisfy the *bona fide residence* or *physical presence* rules may deduct certain expenses for living abroad. The total deductions for such expenses may not exceed net foreign source earned income and are deductible from gross income. Resident aliens living overseas may also qualify for Section 913 deductions but generally only if they meet the "physical presence" test.

Cost-of-Living Differential A deduction will be allowed for an amount by which the cost of living at a foreign tax home location exceeds the general cost of living for the United States metropolitan area (other than Alaska) having the highest cost of living. The deduction is to be measured by tables issued periodically by the IRS. It is to be computed on a daily basis for the period during which the expatriate meets either the bona fide or physical presence test and has a foreign tax home. The expatriate's family size and the cost of living for a family whose income is equal to a government employee grade GS-14, Step 1, (which is currently $34,713) are other relevant factors used in determining the cost-of-living tables.

There is no requirement that an employee actually be paid a cost-of-living allowance to qualify for this deduction.

Excess Housing Expenses The deduction for foreign housing expenses is limited to the excess of reasonable expenses paid or incurred during the taxable year by or on behalf of an employee, his spouse, and his dependents for housing in a

---

*The material in "Deductions for Expenses of Living Abroad" was first published in the Arthur Young Client Memorandum "1978 Tax Legislation Provision Applicable to U.S. Expatriates," copyright © 1978 by Arthur Young & Co. Further material has been reprinted in part from "Taxation of U.S. Expatriates" as amended to take account of the provisions of the "Technical Corrections Act, 1979," copyright © 1980 by Arthur Young & Co. Use of this material is by permission of Arthur Young & Co.

foreign country over the employee's "base housing amount." The base housing amount concept is designed to ensure that only the foreign housing expenses which exceed the cost of average U.S. housing are deducted. Allowable expenses will generally include utilities, insurance, and other similar expenses, but will not include depreciation, capital acquisition costs, foreign real estate taxes or mortgage interest that would be deductible if the expatriate itemized deductions. Expenses will not be deductible to the extent that they are for "lavish or extravagant" quarters, although this phrase is not defined by the law.

The base housing amount is defined to be 20 percent of the excess of the individual's "housing income" (reduced by properly allocable deductions) over the sum of the (a) individual's actual housing expenses, (b) qualified cost-of-living differential, (c) qualified schooling expenses, (d) qualified home leave travel expenses, and (e) qualified hardship area deduction. In general, the deduction will be limited to only one tax home. However, in the event that the employee maintains a separate household for his spouse and dependents in addition to his tax home because of adverse living conditions and his tax home is located in a hardship area, the base housing amount for the household maintained at the tax home will be deemed to be zero, and the housing deduction will be allowed with respect to the expenses of both homes. An individual will qualify for this deduction only during those periods when (a) his tax home is in a foreign country, and (b) he is not excluding housing costs for housing furnished for the employer's convenience, unless the employee maintains a separate household for his spouse and dependents due to adverse living conditions.

The potential benefit to be derived from the housing expense deduction may be less than initially apparent, because the base housing amount reduces the actual housing expense and can be substantial. The starting point for measuring the base housing amount is the expatriate's housing income, including tax reimbursements, foreign post premiums, amounts in excess of allowable expenses of living abroad, bonuses, certain stock option gains, etc. For example, assume that an individual with a base salary of $30,000 holds an overseas position which provides $40,000 of allowances and reimbursements, and housing and qualified expenses of living abroad are $25,000. The housing deduction will be limited to the housing expenses in excess of 20 percent of $45,000, or $9,000.

Schooling Expenses A deduction is allowed for all reasonable expenses for education of a dependent in a foreign country from kindergarten through twelfth grade in a United States-type school. Deductible expenses include tuition, fees, books, local transportation, and other expenses that are required by the school. Where a United States-type school is not within a reasonable commuting distance of the foreign tax home, transportation and room and board will be deductible. Reasonable commuting distance is defined as the distance that can be covered within one hour by car or available water transportation. The employee could send a dependent to a school in the United States if a United States-type school is not available within a reasonable commuting distance of the foreign tax home.

If there is a United States-type school within a reasonable commuting distance of the tax foreign home and the taxpayer chooses to use a different school, a deduction will be allowed to the extent that it does not exceed the deduction allowable if a school within such a commuting distance were used. (Note: A U.S.-type school is defined by the IRS as one whose curriculum is (1) taught in English, (2) is comparable to that offered by accredited schools in the United States, and (3) would qualify the student for graduation if he transferred to a U.S. school.)

Home Leave Travel Expenses An expatriate is allowed to deduct reasonable amounts actually expended for the transportation of himself, spouse, and dependents between the foreign tax home and the individual's present or most recent principal residence in the United States, or if the individual has no principal residence, to the nearest port of entry in the continental United States outside Alaska or Hawaii unless he elects to use these states as the nearest U.S. port of entry. A deduction will be allowed only with respect to one round trip per person for each continuous twelve-month period abroad. Travel expenses do not include meals and lodging en route or after arrival in the United States.

Reasonable transportation expenses by air is generally defined as the lowest coach or economy fare offered during the calendar month in which the transportation is furnished.

Hardship Area Deduction Employees working in a hardship area are allowed a deduction limited to $5,000 per year computed on a daily basis. To qualify, the employee's tax home must be in an area designated by the secretary of state as a hardship post where U.S. government employees would qualify for a post differential of 15 percent or more of salary, i.e., where living conditions are extraordinarily difficult and unhealthy, or excessive physical hardships exist. Hardship areas currently do not include any locations in Western Europe and North America other than the Northwest Territories of Canada and Belfast in the United Kingdom.

Income Earned by Individuals in Certain Camps Citizens of the United States who are bona fide residents of a foreign country or countries and citizens or residents of the United States who are physically present in a foreign country or countries for 510 days in any eighteen-month period, and in either case reside in a camp located in a hardship area, may elect to exclude up to $20,000 annually from earned income and the value of meals and lodging provided by or on behalf of the employer. The exclusion will be computed on a daily basis with each day of residence in a camp providing an exclusion of approximately $55.

Generally, a camp has been defined to be substandard housing which is:

1. provided by an employer for its convenience because the employee renders services in a remote area where satisfactory housing is not available on the open market;
2. located close to the employee's work location; and
3. furnished in a common area not available to the public which normally accommodates ten or more employees.

If the camp exclusion is elected, an individual will not be entitled to the deduction for certain expenses of living abroad and must reduce foreign taxes available for credit or deduction to the extent such taxes are allocable to the $20,000 earned income exclusion. However, it is no longer required that the individual reduce his moving expense deduction by the amount allocable to the exclusion.

An individual may elect not to have the hardship area exclusion apply for a tax year. The election is made on Form 2555, which is filed with the return. It is effective only for the tax year in which the return is filed. It can be revoked.

Moving Expenses Limits on certain deductible moving expenses, under the 1978 legislation, have been increased. The specific limit for the cost of a trip to the new employment location to search for a new residence and for meals and lodging while occupying temporary housing during a period of ninety consecutive days (up from thirty days) has been increased from $1,500 to $4,500. The overall limit for the foregoing expenses as well as expenses related to the sale and purchase of a residence or lease has been increased from $3,000 to $6,000. These increased limits now apply to initial moves overseas and moves between foreign countries but *not* to moves back to the United States or its possessions. Reasonable costs incurred for storing personal effects during the overseas assignment are deductible.

Taxpayers who return to the United States due to retirement or to the death of an individual who was working overseas will be allowed the same deductions as a taxpayer moving within the United States in connection with employment and the higher limits described above will not apply.

Sale of Principal Residence A taxpayer whose tax home is located outside the United States after the sale of a principal residence may defer the gain on the sale by reinvesting in a new residence within a period of up to four years after sale of the old residence. This provision suspends the previous period of eighteen months in the case of a purchase of an existing house and twenty-four months in the case of construction of a new house. The suspension of the eighteen or twenty-four month time period ends when the taxpayer's tax home ceases to be located outside the United States.

Under the Revenue Act of 1978, taxpayers aged fifty-five and over may make a one-time election to exclude up to $100,000 of gain on the sale of a principal residence after July 26, 1978. To qualify, the taxpayer must have owned and occupied the principal residence for three out of the previous five years.

Rental of Personal Residence The vacation home rules added by the 1976 act disallowed certain deductions in excess of rental income if the taxpayer used the property as a personal residence for more than the greater of fourteen days or 10 percent of the rental days in a year. The provision frequently had the unintended effect of limiting the deductions allowable to an expatriate regarding the rental of his U.S. home in the years of expatriation and repatriation. For taxable years beginning after December 31, 1975, the Revenue Act of 1978 provides that the deductions will not be limited where taxpayers use property as their principal residence immediately preceding or following a period in which the property is rented to unrelated parties for a specified period. Thus, taxpayers who were affected by this provision in 1976 and 1977 should consider the filing of refund claims.

Meals and Lodging of Dependents   Prior to the act, meals and lodging could be excluded only to the extent that they were supplied to the employee for the convenience of the employer. The act provides that meals and lodging provided to the employee's spouse and dependents may also be excluded in certain circumstances.

Standard Deduction   Beginning in 1978, the standard deduction, now known as the zero bracket amount, may be claimed by all expatriates.

Working Spouses   Households in which both spouses are employed overseas and that meet either the bona fide residence or physical presence test will be entitled to claim deductions for expenses of living abroad or the camp treatment. Regulations have been issued by the Treasury Department dealing with the application of these provisions where both husband and wife have foreign earned income.

Nonresident Alien Status for Joint Return   The 1976 act provided that a nonresident alien married to a citizen or resident of the United States may elect to be taxed as a resident of the United States, thereby permitting the couple to file a joint return. It required the couple to qualify for the election on the due date of the return. For taxable years beginning after the calendar year 1975, married couples must qualify for the election on the last day of their taxable year. As a result of this provision, affected taxpayers should consider the filing of refund claims.

Withholding   Wages subject to withholding will not include remuneration to the extent that it is reasonable to believe the employee will receive a corresponding deduction for expenses of living abroad or will qualify for the camp exclusion. The change in the definition of wages, as it relates to expenses of living abroad, is applicable to remuneration paid after the enactment of the act. The camp exclusion, however, can be considered with effect from January 1, 1978.

Tax Counseling and Compliance

It should by now be apparent to the expatriate administrator that the preparation of expatriate returns is a complex and multifaceted skill. Since it is not humanly possible for the expatriate administrator to be conversant with worldwide tax laws, most companies designate a public accounting firm to prepare all expatriates' returns. There are a number of international CPA firms now engaged in this business who will not only prepare the required tax returns, but also help you in the administration of your tax equalization policies.

While it could be argued that filing of tax returns is inherently the responsibility of each employee, the expatriate is an international ambassador of your company. Any failure or negligence on his part when reporting or paying his taxes may result in unfavourable publicity for the company. In addition, your company will probably be responsible for any penalties and interest that may be levied against evaders. For these two reasons there has been a decided trend in the last three years for companies to reimburse the total cost of having expatriate income tax returns prepared both in the home country and especially in the work country. Of course, there are limitations, the most common being that any significant income tax preparation expenses associated with noncompany source income will be shared by the employee.

Tax Equalization Salary Deduction

As I have said previously, the most popular approach to expatriate tax administration is "tax equalization." Under this approach, the employee's tax liabilities (home country and work country) are added together and reduced by an amount equivalent to what the employee normally would have paid in taxes had he not gone overseas. The remainder is the company's liability. To implement the tax equalization concept, you need to do the following:

1. Generate and administer a *hypothetical* tax, which is an estimate of the employee's normal home country tax on company source income. Since many expatriates find that their tax liabilities actually decrease while overseas, most major companies require that an estimated tax be withheld each month (whether required by law or not). This is done to prevent an expatriate receiving a tax windfall in both countries as would be the case under the old "tax protection" concept. This in turn eliminates the problem of trying to get expatriates to go to high tax countries by ensuring all personnel are treated the same whether they are assigned to high or low tax areas.

2. Keep the employee "whole" from a cash flow standpoint during the year, understanding that he will probably be subject to mandatory withholding on taxable income at the same time in both the work country and the home country. This may mean an ongoing program of periodic tax reimbursements or cash advancements during the tax year.

3. Ascertain the employee's legitimate tax liability in both the home and work countries at the conclusion of each tax year.

4. Estimate the employee's tax liability had he not gone on assignment.

5. Generate a tax reconciliation at the end of each home-country tax year. The purpose of this computation is to balance all the various tax liabilities, withholding, and payments during the year, and to arrive at the final cash transfer between the employee and the company, so the employee neither gains nor loses.

Before we proceed with details of how to administer each of the above five steps, please study carefully the following tax equalization example until you feel comfortable with the concept.

Tax Equalization Example

Assumptions:
- U.S. expatriate, married, two children
- Base salary: $30,000
- Allowances (LCD, ISP, position allowance, etc.): $17,156
- Effective foreign tax rate (country A: 30%; country B: 5%)
- Hypothetical U.S. tax on base (15% standard deduction, no limit): $4,700
- Theoretical tax (tax employee would have incurred had he not left the United States): $4,505

	Work Country	
	Country A (High Tax)	Country B (Low Tax)
Foreign Tax		
Base Salary	$30,000	$30,000
Allowances	17,156	17,156
Hypothetical Tax	(4,700)	(4,700)
(salary is reduced by this amount)		
Income subject to foreign tax	42,456	42,456
Tax Rate	30%	5%
Foreign Tax	12,736	2,122
Reimbursement to Employee	$12,736	$ 2,122
(Employee Pays Tax)		
U.S. Income Tax		
Base Salary	$30,000	$30,000
Allowances	17,156	17,156
Hypothetical Tax	(4,700)	(4,700)
Foreign Tax Reimbursement to Employee	12,736	2,122
Other taxable reimbursements	5,650	5,650
(air fares, schooling, etc.)	60,842	50,228

	Work Country	
	Country A (High Tax)	Country B (Low Tax)
Gross Taxable Income	60,842	50,228
Section 913 allowable deductions*	(18,300)	(20,400)
Exemptions (4)	(4,000)	(4,000)
Itemized deductions	(1,400)	(1,400)
(net of zero bracket)		
Adjusted Taxable Income	37,142	24,428
U.S. Tax (Before Credits)	$ 8,997	$ 4,456
Foreign Tax Credit	(12,736)	(2,122)
U.S. Income Tax	$ - 0 -	$ 2,334

Theoretical U.S. Income Tax

(Tax employee would have incurred had he not left the U.S.)		
Base Salary	$30,000	$30,000
Personal Exemptions (4)	(4,000)	(4,000)
Other Deductions	(1,400)	(1,400)
(greater of actual deductions, maximum allowable standard deduction or last 2-3 year average)		
Taxable Income	$24,600	$24,600
U.S. Income Tax	$ 4,505	$ 4,505

Tax Equalization Calculations

A. *Total Taxes Incurred*		
Foreign Taxes	$12,736	$ 2,122
U.S. Income Taxes	0	2,334
Total Taxes	$12,736	$ 4,456
B. *Employee Tax Status*		
Hypothetical Tax Withheld	$ 4,700	$ 4,700
Theoretical Tax Liability	4,505	4,505
Tax Over (Under) Withheld	$ 195	$ 195

---

*Assumes same IRS cost-of-living deduction in both examples.

	Work Country	
	Country A (High Tax)	Country B (Low Tax)
C. *Tax Equalization*		
Total Taxes Incurred	$12,736	$ 4,456
Payments to Employee for Tax	(12,736)	(2,122)
Taxes Remaining to Be Paid	$ 0	$ 2,334
Taxes Over (Under) Withheld	195	195**
Reimbursement to Employee to Pay Remaining Tax Liability	$ 195*	$ 2,529

Summary of Cash Payments

A. *Employee Payments*		
To hypothetical withholding	$ 4,700	$ 4,700
To company for under-withholding	(195)	0
To government for tax liability	0	(195)
Total taxes paid (theoretical tax)	$ 4,505	$ 4,505
B. *Company Payments*		
To employee for foreign tax	$12,736	$ 2,122
To employee for U.S. tax	0	2,529
From employee as reimbursement	195	0
From employee withholding	(4,700)	(4,700)
Cost to company	$ 8,231	$ (49)

---

*Employee reimbursed by company.
**Portion of tax liability employee pays directly to government.

Note: It is recommended that each of the above tax computations and returns (home country and work country) be prepared by a professional tax accounting firm to assure an accurate, complete return and one which reflects the lowest possible tax.

Your first observation should be that in the above example, as in all tax equalization computations, the employee is kept *whole,* and any gain or loss is absorbed by the company. The employee pays an equitable amount to *someone,* either the government or the company, in the form of a hypothetical tax withholding, an amount of money equal to his normal home tax burden of $4,505. The company, on the other hand, either gains or loses depending on the country of assignment. Since many companies send their employees to countries where the tax bite is lower than in the United States, this technique has helped defray other costs associated with sending an employee overseas.

IMPLEMENTING A TAX EQUALIZATION PROGRAM

Now that you have acquainted yourself with the philosophy and mechanics of tax equalization and understand the calculations involved, I will now attempt to expand on my previous outline of actions required to complete the five-step approach.

Step 1: Calculating a Hypothetical Tax

The calculation of a hypothetical tax for the U.S. can generally be done by the expatriate administrator using the tax tables published annually by the Internal Revenue Service. The administrator first determines the number of tax dependents and reduces the employee's gross annual income by the actual number of tax exemptions claimed. The remaining amount is further reduced by an estimated standard/itemized deduction of say 15 percent of base. Having established net taxable income, the following tax table is then referenced to determine the hypothetical tax. For administrative simplicity, you may want to use only the married tax tables.

In the event your company should need information on tax rates for other countries, there are companies who specialize in summarizing the tax laws of all countries and who publish estimates of tax liability by level of income.

Step 2: Tax Reimbursements During the Year

Almost without exception, most countries of the world operate a pay-as-you-earn tax structure and require com-

Married Individual Filing Joint Return
1979 Tax Year

Taxable Income	Tax on Column 1	Percent on Excess
$ 3,400 or less	$ 0	14
5,500	294	16
7,600	630	18
11,900	1,404	21
16,000	2,265	24
20,200	3,273	28
24,600	4,505	32
29,900	6,201	37
35,200	8,162	43
45,800	12,720	49
60,000 and over	19,678	50*

*Taxable income over $60,000 is assumed to be taxed at the 50 percent tax rate due to the current tax laws concerning maximum tax.

panies to withhold a monthly amount as a down payment against eventual tax liabilities. Since the expatriate is already paid less than his gross salary because of hypothetical tax withholding, the company will need to either reimburse or loan the employee an amount equivalent to the mandatory government withholding. In addition, the company may wish to gross up the reimbursement by a given factor—say 25 percent—in recognition of the fact that even a reimbursement is regarded as income and must itself be withheld against. It is very important to maintain excellent records of amounts reimbursed to and withheld from your expatriates if you are to reconcile his taxes at the end of the tax year.

Step 3: Determination of the Employee's Legitimate Tax Liability

It is virtually impossible for either an employee or an expatriate administrator to complete the tax returns required for employees on international assignment. The tax laws are far too diverse and complex, and any approach other than to engage a qualified tax consultant will probably result in either an incorrect tax return being submitted or too much tax being paid. In addition, it is not economically feasible for companies to employ tax experts whose job it is to keep up to date on the personal tax laws of all the countries around the world. For these reasons, it is almost a universal rule that an expatriate is required to have his returns prepared by a designated accounting firm both in the work country and home country, as a condition of the overseas assignment. Most companies pay for the preparation of the returns; in many instances, professional tax counsel are able to generate tax savings, often in excess of the fee charged.

Step 4: Estimating the Employee's Normal Home-Country Tax Liability

An integral part of completing the tax equalization equation is determining the employee's normal or theoretical home-country tax liability. This part of the calculation determines what the employee's actual tax liability will be while on assignment and up to what level he will be protected. Because this exercise is a simulation of what would have been, and not what is, the assumptions used to compute the employee's theoretical tax must be as realistic as possible. Rest assured, the employee will scrutinize the calculations as closely as he would his own tax return. The generally accepted approach is to compute a theoretical tax return utilizing only post-expatriate-source income items—i.e., base salary, etc. In other words, compute the tax he would have paid on base salary in the US had he not accepted an expatriate assignment.

At this stage the services of a designated professional accounting firm can be of further value. Assuming that the consultant is already completing the employee's tax return and has all the earnings data, it is both expedient and cost effective to have them calculate the theoretical tax at the same time. Not only does this procedure insure accuracy and fairness, but, if there are any questions on the part of the employee, qualified personnel are readily available to provide competent answers. Most of the calculations are relatively straightforward. The one exception deals with the application of the standard deduction or itemized deductions to arrive at net taxable income. When an employee goes overseas, it is not uncommon for him to sell his residence; thus, mortgage interest, real estate taxes, and other itemized deductions are lost. For this reason, I believe an employee should receive as deductions the greater of: (1) the employee's itemized deduction while on assignment; (2) the maximum allowable standard deduction; or (3) the average deductions claimed by the employee over the last two years prior to expatriation excluding any significant one-off items such as casualty losses, capital gains (losses), etc.

Step 5: Completing a Tax Reconciliation at the End of the Home-Country Tax Year

Once the tax returns have been prepared and the employee's normal tax liability calculated, it is the responsibility of the expatriate administrator to prepare the tax equalization statement. This should be done immediately after tax return preparation so that the reimbursement process takes place before the employee must remit the balance of any taxes owed to the government. There are three items which must be completed as part of the tax equalization calculations:

1. All taxes incurred by the employee, both in the work country and home country, must be totaled.
2. The administrator should determine whether the hypothetical tax withholding exceeded or was less than the expatriate's normal home-country tax liability.

3. The administrator must pull together all the various data that have been prepared and determine what reimbursements, if any, are due the employee.

COMPONENT 5: LIVING COST DIFFERENTIAL

The purpose of providing a living cost differential is strictly to keep the expatriate "whole," that is, to ensure that he neither gains nor loses in his effort to maintain a comparable standard of living in the country of assignment. This differential or allowance should be computed so that the expatriate will be the same as if he had remained at home in terms of purchasing power. I personally prefer the use of the term differential as opposed to "allowance" when communicating with expatriates, thereby reminding the expatriate and others involved in the expatriation process that what we are trying to do is to compensate for the incremental costs or difference between the home country and the work country.

From a technical standpoint, a living cost differential (LCD) is really a composite of two components—namely a goods and services differential, and a quarters differential.

A goods and services differential is an allowance which is intended to compensate for the incremental cost of purchasing a given market basket of consumable goods and services at a given point in time in the work country. This allowance, added to that part of the expatriate's base salary normally spent on goods and services in the home country, should approximate his work country living costs.

A quarters differential is an allowance which is designed to compensate the employee for the cost of housing in the foreign location in excess of what he might reasonably have been expected to pay in the home country. Again, this allowance is not intended to compensate for the total cost of foreign housing, only the incremental cost.

Expatriates generally expect and perceive the costs of maintaining an American life-style to be higher in the work country than at home—and most of the time they are. It is possible, however, that the employee will find that the cost of goods and services is less, while the cost of quarters is significantly above the cost of his home-country housing, or vice versa. If this occurs, it is normal practice for the two components to be netted. Notwithstanding the above, in no case is the expatriate given a negative living cost differential, i.e., if both goods and services and housing is cheaper, the expatriate should simply receive zero LCD.

Goods and Services Differential

How do we ascertain whether the work-country living costs are greater or smaller? How do we know if the expatriate's standard of living is improving or deteriorating? Since our standard of living is determined primarily by our after-tax income, a change in either base salary or tax burden may be significant. Living cost differentials are designed to work with the expatriate's net after-tax income to provide the moneys required to maintain a satisfactory living standard.

Assuming that the employee's base salary and tax rate is comparable to that of the home country, the next step is to acquire cost-of-living indexes from a reputable consulting firm who market this data after having conducted carefully controlled surveys in each country. We covered briefly what items are typically included under the title goods and services in the section on base salary.

Cost of Living Indices

Experience in the expatriate field has taught me that despite a general reluctance to understand pricings, weightings, etc., a resolute expatriate administrator will familiarize himself with the techniques and assumptions that go into deriving indexes. Not only will this help him explain to an expatriate why an index increased or decreased, but will also serve as the basis for understanding the theory which makes up the balance sheet concept. It is really very simple. To help illustrate, I will make some simple assumptions, which make it easy to follow, but which should in no way detract from the credibility of the concept. Please for a second, assume that there are two countries—the United States and Germany—and the only good or service consumed is bread. We will for illustration purposes assume that we are talking about a United States expatriate to Germany.

Example: Principles of COL Indices

Assumptions:

- U.S. expatriate to Germany.
- Surveyed commodity: bread.
- Exchange rate is 2 Dmarks to the U.S. dollar.
- Bread costs $2 in the United States and 6 Dmarks in Germany (the bread is the same size and type)

$$\text{COL Index (U.S. to Germany)} = \frac{\text{Cost of German bread in dollars}}{\text{Cost of U.S. bread in dollars}}$$

As you can see, before being able to compare the relative prices, you first have to convert the price of German bread to dollars, since that is the currency in which the home country loaf of bread is expressed.

	U.S. Loaf of Bread	*German Loaf of Bread*
Cost	$2	6 Dmarks
Exchange Rate		$1 = 2 Dmarks
Cost in Dollars	$2	$3

COL Index = ($3 ÷ $2) = 1.5, or 150 on an index base of 100

We can assume at this point that the cost of bread in Germany is 50 percent more than in the United States if an individual is compensated in dollars and must convert the dollars to Dmarks to buy the German bread. This is a valid assumption, because most expatriates want their pay calculated in home-country currency, since they can relate more easily to its value.

In the above example, we expect the U.S. expatriate to take his pay calculated in dollars and, on the free market, convert them to Dmarks and purchase the same quantity of German bread as he would American bread in the states. As you may now begin to see, any relative cost differential is influenced by the exchange rate the expatriate receives for the currency he is paid. Let's look briefly at what the index becomes when the relative cost of bread in the two countries stays constant, but the dollar strengthens to $1 = 3$ Dmarks.

	U.S. Loaf of Bread	*German Loaf of Bread*
Cost	$2	6 Dmarks
Exchange Rate		$1 = 3 Dmarks
Cost in Dollars	$2	$2

COL Index = ($2 ÷ $2) = 1.0, or 100 on an index base of 100

The cost is now the same in the United States and Germany. Of course, this example is overly simplistic, but I believe it illustrates that a change in the relative cost of goods and services can be influenced as much or more by changing exchange rates as by the price of the items in local currency.

Before we conclude our discussions on the cost-of-living indices, I want to reiterate that the COL index is almost always only a reflection of relative costs for consumable items such as food, clothing, entertainment, gasoline, etc. Items such as automobiles and living quarters costs are not normally reflected in the index. Costs for quarters will be discussed later. The important thing is that you understand that a COL index is used to equate one unit of home country purchasing power to "x" units of work country purchasing power.

For example, if we assume an individual normally spends $500 per month on goods and services in his home country, the United States, and that the COL index is 150 at an exchange rate of $1 equals 2 Dmarks for the United States to Germany, it is reasonable to expect that at one point in time, he needs $750 per month ($500 x 1.5) to have the same purchasing power in Germany (Dmarks 1,500).

Note that I specified the exchange rate at the point in time the index was surveyed. The reason, of course, has to do with the fact that the exchange rate assumption is a key factor in the determination of the index.

Working with Cost-of-Living Indices

There are a variety of sources from which you can obtain cost-of-living indices. In addition to the U.S. State Department and consultants who employ pricing agents around the world to assist expatriate administrators, you may want to conduct some surveys yourself. Regardless of the source, the index you acquire will be determined at a given exchange rate at a fixed point in time, and, to be meaningful at any subsequent point in time, it must be adjusted to comprehend the change in exchange rate. Let's refer back to my examples on the United States to German bread indices.

Let's assume that the exchange rate is $1 equals 2 Dmarks and the COL index is 150. Going back to the previous example, this meant that $500 in the United States was equivalent to 1,500 Dmarks of purchasing power in Germany. We also saw that when the exchange rate changed to $1 equals 3 Dmarks, the index fell to 100; but $500 in the U.S. was still equivalent to 1,500 Dmarks of purchasing power in Germany. The trick is to take an index, assuming the relative inflation rate between the two countries is minimal, and adjust the available index to comprehend the exchange rate change that has occurred since it was surveyed.

The method to do this is as follows:
- At time zero, when the exchange rate is $1 = 2 Dmarks, we calculate the index to be 150.
- We check the exchange rate one month later and it is then $1 = 3 Dmarks.

- Adjusted Index = Old Index x $\dfrac{\text{Old Exchange Rate}}{\text{New Exchange Rate}}$
- Adjusted Index = 150 x (2.0 ÷ 3.0) = 100

If you will refer back to the example based on bread, you will find that we have arrived at the same answer. Thus, you can see this approach will allow you to keep your indices compatible with changing exchange rates.

Calculating a Goods and Services Differential

Now is the time to consolidate the concepts and techniques we have discussed, in order to calculate the appropriate goods and services differential for an expatriate overseas. The first is that of spendable income. Spendable income, as you will recall, is the portion of base salary the employee normally spends on goods and services in the US. The reason this concept is so important is that it is only against this portion of the base rate that we want to apply the cost-of-living index. Thus, if we take an employee's income (base salary), determine what portion is spendable income, and factor this portion by some cost-of-living index, we should be able to determine what the living costs will be in the work country. The formula to do this is as follows:

$$\text{G\&S Differential} = \text{Base Salary}$$
$$\times \text{Spendable Income Factor} \times$$
$$\frac{(\text{Index} - 100)}{100}$$

To see exactly how the formula works, let's run through

an example using some familiar assumptions and utilizing the tables found in the section on components of base salary.

Assumptions:
● U.S. expatriate to Germany
● Expatriate is married with two children
● Hypothetical cost-of-living index is 150 at present exchange rate of $1 = 2 Dmarks (Note: this is not a true index for the United States to Germany. It is probably closer to 200 at time of going to press, but I have used 150 to be consistent with earlier examples.)
● Base salary is $2,500 per month or $30,000 per year

G&S Differential = Base Salary	$2,500 per month
× Spendable Income Factor	.565
× Index $\frac{(150 - 100)}{100}$	$\frac{.50}{\$706.25 \text{ per month}}$
	$8,475 per year

(Note: The spendable income factor for a base salary of $30,000 per year is .50. This must be adjusted by a factor of 1.13 because two children accompany the expatriate.)

The above hypothetical example indicates that, for the given set of assumptions, you should provide this expatriate with $8,475 per year in goods and services differential for him to maintain a comparable standard of living in the work country. Again, we should not forget nor let the expatriate forget that this is a differential, and has to be added to his normal stateside goods-and-services budget (spendable income) in order to meet his work-country living costs. Too frequently, expatriates feel they should be able to live solely off the differential. In this example, the expatriate is expected to spend $25,425 per year in the work country for goods and services; this includes $16,950 normally appropriated from base salary in his own country, plus the $8,475 differential that we calculated above.

Again, underlying our calculations is the belief that the expatriate or the company will convert this dollar amount into local currency to spend in Germany. At an exchange rate of $1 = 2 Dmarks, this would yield $50,850 Dmarks per year to purchase the necessary goods and services. The common practice in industry is to operate a split payroll which pays the employee his spendable income and any G&S differentials in the work country, thus (1) the expatriate is relieved of having to convert his dollars to work-country currency each month; and (2) he is paid locally the correct amount required to live comfortably without building excess cash reserves outside his home country.

Let's take a second before we leave this subject to reconsider what our objectives were and whether we achieved them. Let's presume that while the expatriate is overseas, our hypothetical exchange rate starts to change and, as of today, the rate is $1 = 3 Dmarks. Using our formula to update the index, we find that the adjusted index is now 100, thus *no* differential is required. We would now expect the expatriate to spend only the spendable income portion of his base rate in the work country; or $16,950 per year. Assuming the expatriate or the company will convert this amount at the current exchange rate, the employee will find he still receives 50,850 Dmarks ($16,950 x 3) to live on in the work country. If your company does not operate a split payroll, one of your most difficult tasks will be to communicate to the expatriate that in work-country currency (the currency he is spending), he is still "whole," even though his compensation expressed in dollars has decreased.

Quarters Differential

The first thing that impresses (or depresses) an expatriate upon leaving the United States is the heterogeneity of housing. It is amazing how building techniques and designs vary from country to country, resulting in a miscellany of possible quarters environments. The bottom line is that it is almost impossible for an expatriate to find housing in the work country exactly comparable to that found in the United States. This fact, compounded by the inherent desire of the expatriate to live in quality housing and local managements' desire to preserve profits, leaves the expatriate administrator with somewhat of a dilemma. He is expected to produce equitable housing or quarters differentials without the digital accuracy of goods and services indices.

Since housing, above all else, is judged to be the biggest expatriate satisfier or dissatisfier and is considered to have a major impact on job performance, I believe it is prudent to suggest that most housing cost estimates are generous rather than austere. This is probably as it should be, since the natural market forces which control the housing market in the United States are really not applicable in a foreign work environment. Whereas in the United States the quality of housing is determined primarily by income level, expatriates in a foreign work location tend to favor community living and settle for the same type of housing independent of income level.

There are a variety of approaches currently being used by companies to calculate a quarters differential; this is primarily due to the degree of subjectivity involved in estimating comparable work-country quarters costs incurred by an average employee. The balance sheet concept favors an approach whereby the employee is paid an ongoing differential which is equal to the employee's allowable cost of quarters in the work country offset by an estimate of what we think his stateside expenditure would have been at home (referred to later as "home-country housing cost estimate.") This stateside estimate is based on government published data that compute average quarters costs for various income brackets. It is not unique for each individual. It is important that the administrator obtain the latest data available on both U.S. and foreign housing costs and that this data be kept up to date. There are consulting firms which, for a fee, will supply you with an estimate of what they think is a reasonable work-country housing cost. In addition, you can contact the State Department in Washington, and they will send you information on both domestic housing figures and what they provide their employees overseas.

Calculating the Quarters Cost

Before we delve into the formulas required to calculate the differential, it is appropriate to take the time to discuss how consultants determine the quarters cost in the work country. The approach most frequently used is for the data gatherer or pricing agent to visit the locality where expatriates are actually living and survey a cross-section of property normally leased by Americans in conjunction with visits to local real estate offices. In this way it is possible to develop typical housing costs for expatriates at various income levels. Please remember that the data are gathered in local currency. The output of this effort is a matrix of work-country quarters costs relative to the base salary or income of the employee. Let's assume that the data gatherer has determined that the average married American living in Munich whose base salary is between $28,000 and $35,000 typically spends about 20,000 Dmarks annually on housing. There are, of course, other living cost estimates for other income levels, but we will, for simplicity purposes, deal only with this data point.

Once the cost has been verified, the consultants convert this value (Dm 20,000) into dollars at the current exchange rate. For example, we will assume the exchange rate at the time of the survey was $1 = 2 Dmarks. Thus, the cost expressed in dollars is $10,000 annually. You will note that the cost expressed in dollars could be more or less, depending solely upon the exchange rate. For this reason, any time you work with overseas quarters costs expressed in dollars, be sure you know what exchange rate was used at the time the survey was conducted so that you can adjust the differential in line with subsequent exchange rate perturbations. The method for accomplishing this is the same as for adjusting goods and services indices.

Calculating the Quarters Differential

The formula we will be using to calculate the differential is as follows:

$$\begin{array}{c}\text{Quarters} \\ \text{Differential}\end{array} = \begin{array}{c}\text{Adjusted Overseas} \\ \text{Quarters Cost}\end{array} - \begin{array}{c}\text{Home Country Housing} \\ \text{Cost Estimate}\end{array}$$

As you can see, there are three individual components which come into play when calculating the differential. We will address each one individually and then develop an easy example. The example assumptions are the same as used previously:

Assumptions:
- U.S. expatriate to Germany
- Expatriate is married with two children
- Base salary is $2,500 per month, or $30,000 per year
- Quarters cost estimate is $10,000 per year at $1 = 2 Dmarks
- Current exchange rate is $1 = 2 Dmarks

Adjusted Overseas Quarters Cost

Adjusted Overseas Quarters Cost in dollars =

$$\left[\begin{array}{c}\text{Overseas} \\ \text{Quarters Cost} \\ \text{in Dollars}\end{array} \times \frac{\text{Survey Exch. Rate}}{\text{Current Exch. Rate}} \right] \begin{array}{c}\text{Family Size} \\ \text{Factor}\end{array}$$

Referring to the section on base salary, we estimate that married employees with two children spend 1.13 times the amount a married employee with no children spends on quarters.

$$\text{Adjusted Quarters Cost} = \left[\$10,000 \times \frac{2.0}{2.0} \right] \times 1.13 = \$11,300$$

Home Country Housing Cost Estimate

Home Country Housing Cost Estimate =

$$\left[\begin{array}{l} \text{Home Country} \\ \text{Quarters Spendable} \times \\ \text{Income} \end{array} \begin{array}{l} \text{Base} \\ \text{Salary} \end{array} \right] \begin{array}{l} \text{Family Size} \\ \text{Factor} \end{array}$$

You will recall from the section on components of base salary that married Americans making between \$20,000 and \$30,000 normally spend about 21 percent of their base salary on quarters. Utilizing this estimate in our equation yields the following:

$$\text{Home Country Housing Cost Estimate} = (0.21 \times \$30,000) \times 1.13 = \$7,119$$

Final Calculations

We will again state the equation and then plug in the values we have calculated for each component.

$$\text{Quarters Differential} = \text{Adjusted Quarters Cost} - \text{Home Country Housing Cost Estimate}$$

Quarters Differential = \$11,300 − \$7,119 = \$4,181

We are now at the point where we can finalize our living cost differential calculation. The sum of the previous components results in the following differential:

Goods and Services Differential	\$ 8,475 per year
Quarters Differential	4,181 per year
Living Cost Differential	\$12,656 per year

COMPONENT 6: POSITION ALLOWANCE

Keeping the expatriate whole and enabling him to enjoy the same standard of living abroad as he would have enjoyed at home is the key to the balance sheet concept. However, if the resultant standard is significantly below that of his work-country peers (or possibly subordinates), he could be unnecessarily embarrassed. This is especially true if the expatriate, because of required business and social engagements, has to interface with these peers at the same social level. A lower standard of living (albeit whole in terms of his home country) could be humiliating to the expatriate manager and create financial difficulties. It would also be a poor reflection on the company.

There are a few locations in the world where the local pay scales are significantly higher for a given job than they are in the United States. Even with expatriate benefits and allowances added, the bottom line of the expatriate package (ignoring the foreign service premium) is still considerably less than what a local national earns net after tax for the same job.

The position allowance is calculated such that on an after-tax basis and discounting foreign service premium, the expatriate will be no worse off financially than his work-country peer. Since comparing actual earnings levels of individuals in two locations is burdensome and exact profile matches are seldom possible, we must compare relative positions within a job grade rate schedule. Perhaps we can illustrate using our example of the American to Germany, but first let us examine the formula:

$$\left[\begin{array}{l} \text{Work Country} \\ \text{Equivalent} \\ \text{Base Rate} \end{array} - \begin{array}{l} \text{Work-Country} \\ \text{Tax} \end{array} \right] -$$

$$\left[\begin{array}{l} \text{Expatriate} \\ \text{Base} \\ \text{Salary} \end{array} + \begin{array}{l} \text{Living} \\ \text{Cost} \\ \text{Differential} \end{array} - \begin{array}{l} \text{Hypothetical} \\ \text{H/C Tax} \\ \text{Withholding} \end{array} \right] = \text{Position Allowance}$$

The position allowance must be greater than zero. If the formula produces a negative number it simply means that it costs more to maintain a U.S. standard of living in the work country; a zero is then entered on the package. Remember, our goal is to provide the expatriate with either the same standard of living as at home or raise it to that of his local peers, whichever is higher. We never lower his standard of living to below that of the United States since to do so would probably dissuade the employee from accepting the assignment in the first place.

Let's again assume that our expatriate is paid $30,000 annual salary and that he is at 95 percent of the job grade midpoint on the U.S. rate schedule (e.g., minimum $25,200, midpoint $31,500, maximum $37,800). His LCD is $12,656 and hypothetical tax withholding is $4,700. This results in an expatriate earnings after tax and discounting foreign service premium of $37,956. If we convert this to Dmarks at an exchange rate of $1 = Dm2, it equals Dm75,912.

In Germany, an employee of equivalent job grade and at the same relative position in the German rate schedule (i.e., 95 percent of midpoint) might be earning Dm81,500 (e.g., minimum Dm68,560, midpoint Dm85,700, maximum Dm-102,840) less tax of Dm21,000. Applying these numbers to our equation and converting the U.S. numbers to Dmarks, again at $1 = Dm2, we get:

$$(Dm\ 81,500 - Dm\ 21,000) - (Dm\ 60,000 + 25,312 - 9,400) = -15,412$$

The position differential in this instance would be zero since a negative number resulted. If it had been positive, we would have paid it to the expatriate to achieve our objective of establishing an earnings level which, as a minimum, is comparable with his work-country peers.

PAYING THE EXPATRIATE

The objective behind each of the various calculations we have performed is to arrive at a compensation package that permits the expatriate to live overseas without deterioration of his living standard and to pay him an incentive premium for working overseas. The expatriate package we have constructed for the employee will do this. The following is the suggested expatriate package format we discussed at the beginning of this chapter, but with the numbers calculated in the previous sections entered in.

Expatriate Compensation Package
(Personal and Confidential)

Employee Data:

Name John Expatriate	Employee Number 1000	Effective Date 9/8/80
Assignment Work Location Munich, Germany	Normal Work Location Dallas, Texas	
Work Assignment Manufacturing Engineer		Job Grade 20
Marital Status Married	Number Children with Expatriate 2	Total Number Tax Dependents 4

Compensation Summary:

	Annual Compensation $
1. Base Salary $2,500 per month	$30,000
2. Hypothetical Tax	(4,700)
3. International Service Premium	4,500
4. Hardship Premium	0
5. Living Cost Differential	12,656
6. Position Allowance	0
7. Net Compensation Estimate (After Tax)	$42,456

Utilizing this format, we can document for record purposes and for pay purposes the hypothetical tax, international service premiums, hardship premium, and living cost differential needed to provide a sustainable package. The next step is to determine how much of the employee's net compensation should be paid in the work country and how much in dollars to his U.S. bank account.

The general rule which should be followed, if at all possible, is that the employee should be paid in local currency his home-country spendable income (goods and services, normal home-country quarters cost) and any living cost differentials provided. Looking back over our calculations, the following is a summary of what the employee should be paid overseas:

Spendable income (goods and services)	$16,950
($30,000 × .50 × 1.13)	
Home country quarters cost	7,119
($30,000 × .21 × 1.13)	
Living cost differential	12,656
Position allowance	0
Overseas pay	$36,725

We can now complete the bottom of our suggested expatriate package form as follows:

Payroll Split:

	Per Month	Per Year
Home Country Pay	$ 478	$ 5,731
Work Country Pay	3,060	36,725
Net Compensation	3,538	42,456
Exchange Rate	$1 = 2 Dmarks	
Work Country Pay (Local Currency)	DM 6,120	DM 73,450

BENEFITS

For the purpose of inclusion under the various benefit programs, all U.S. expatriates should be considered as employees of the parent U.S. company and should continue participation in the domestic programs. Any deductions for employee costs can be made from the U.S.-paid portion of their salary. Eligible earnings for continued participation normally include base pay, international service premium, and hardship premium, if any. All other additions are purely cost-of-living adjustments and are not true earnings.

Where statutory participation in foreign governmental plans necessitates duplicate contributions, the company should reimburse the expatriate for the work-country costs.

Temporary Assignments

Many companies do not have a formal policy covering assignments of less than one year, consequently, when one of their employees is asked to go on a special assignment for two or three months, he is simply given some traveler's checks to cover reasonable expenditures at the overseas location and asked to remit an expense statement when he gets back. Other companies, which perhaps send people overseas on a more frequent basis and for longer durations, will often pay expenses until the employee settles into an apartment or negotiates a long-term occupancy agreement with a hotel, and then revert to a per diem basis to compensate in full for international living costs.

Unlike expatriates who sell or lease their homes and take the family with them, an individual sent for a short spell abroad does not reduce his normal operating expenses here in the United States. Invariably, he retains his house, and his wife and children stay behind; except for a small reduction in the food bill, the ongoing costs in the United States are the same. Therefore, unlike an expatriate package where we apply the equivalent of home-country spendable income and housing against what we pay in the way of overseas differential, for the temporary assignee we need to pay all incremental costs in the majority of cases.

There appears to be no universal trend for handling short-term assignments of less than a year, so the following proposal is my own idea of how it might be structured.

0–30 days—Business Trip (expense account)
0–180 days—Temporary Assignment (per diem)
0–365 days—Short Term Assignment
365 plus days—Expatriate Assignment

BUSINESS TRIPS (0–30 DAYS)

I don't think there is any question that this type of excursion should be handled on an expense account basis even if the duration exceeds 30 days. In most cases, the employee is moving from city to city and any other financial arrangement would be impractical. No additional benefits or premiums are paid to people on expense account.

TEMPORARY ASSIGNMENTS (0–180 DAYS)

Where the intent is for the employee to be out of the country for a period not exceeding six months, I recommend he be paid base salary, a foreign service premium, and a single-status per diem. The company should allow him to return home every 60 days if it is practical to do so (or allow the spouse to visit the foreign location). The employee should continue to be compensated from the United States and be subject to U.S. tax withholding. If there are any foreign tax liabilities—and I doubt there will be for less than 180 days—the company should pay any excess.

SHORT TERM ASSIGNMENTS (0–365 DAYS)

Where the intent is for the employee to be out of the country for a period exceeding six months but not more than a year, I recommend he be paid base salary, an international service premium, and a living cost differential for the estimated additional living costs in the work location (see above for computation of LCD). Most companies would allow the employee's family to join him where it is practical to do so. If the family does not join him, he should receive single status LCD with no deduction for home-country housing cost estimate. He should also be permitted to return home at least every quarter.

Many companies prefer to pay a per diem to all employees assigned overseas for less than a year, factored upwards to comprehend family size if they accompany him. Either way is satisfactory. With regard to taxes, the company should reimburse any U.S. or work-country taxes in excess of a hypothetical home-country tax (estimated tax the employee would have paid on the same base salary had he remained in the United States). If there is a reduction in home-country taxes as a result of the temporary assignment, the employee should remit the difference to the company.

Third Country Nationals (TCNs)

A third country national is a citizen of a country other than either the one in which he is working or the one in which the parent company is located. Traditionally, because of the wide variety of home countries, problems governing personnel in this category are perplexing to say the least, and they are frequently handled on an ad hoc basis without clearcut or defined policies. The age-old question is still being asked—should they receive equal remuneration for doing the same job as an American in a third country? I think not, but there are many who disagree with me. If we accept the fact that economic differences exist between individuals while located in their respective home countries, there should be no obligation to eliminate those economic differences simply because people are on assignment. Provided all employees receive similar inducements in terms of percentage bonuses, and are kept "whole" vis-à-vis their spending power while overseas, I see no reason to create new problems by providing greater inducement to one nationality than to another. In addition, if all employees assigned overseas were to receive the same pay for doing the same job, regardless of national origin, the company would be forced to set its expatriate pay scales at the highest common denominator. This would be very costly, and to my mind, totally unacceptable.

Having said all that, I will itemize the four alternatives which have been most commonly used in compensating third country nationals in recent years:

1. Case-by-case determination, in which the company negotiates with each individual. This works well where only a small number of TCNs are employed and geographical diversity eliminates the opportunity for them to compare packages. For companies that employ large numbers of TCNs, consistency in administration is important and would render this approach inappropriate. This approach also fails to facilitate moves from one assignment to another since each move would require fresh negotiations.

2. Payment of host country rates. When moving an employee from a low base-rate country to a high base-rate country, many companies simply treat the TCN as if he were a local national. By placing him on the host country rate schedule and giving him increases according to local inflation, he is in effect kept "whole" vis-à-vis his local peers. The problem with this approach is that it doesn't work when an employee from a high base-rate country moves to a low base-rate country. The concept also makes it very difficult to repatriate an employee since visibility is lost of his relative position in the home country rate schedule.

3. Compensate expatriates and TCNs equally. Many companies have elected to pay TCNs equal to their American counterparts. This certainly works well when the TCN is from a relatively low base-rate country. But I doubt that many U.S. multinational corporations could convince a Swiss, Belgium, Dutch, French, German, or Brazilian TCN that he should be paid in accordance with U.S. pay scales. (An American working alongside

a German in a third country could conceivably ask to be paid the same as the German). This snowball effect can get very costly and could necessitate the company setting its pay scales at the highest common denominator to satisfy everyone. It also creates further problems in that TCNs from low base-rate countries receive a tremendous inducement and improvement in living standard whereas those from a higher base-rate country receive little or no inducement.

4. Utilize the balance sheet approach. Since many consultant firms have now developed unique third-country spendable income curves and tax tables and have developed indexes based on third country market baskets and weightings, the majority of U.S. companies with whom I have dealings operate a TCN compensation program which parallels the approach used for U.S. expatriates.

—Home-country base salary
—Foreign service premium (percent of base pay)
—Position allowance
—Housing differential (work country cost less home country housing cost estimate)
—Goods and services differential (index from home country to work country applied to home country spendable income)
—Less hypothetcal tax (tax equalization based on equivalent of home country tax on base pay)

The rationale and logic behind each of the above components is exactly the same as described earlier in this chapter, the objective being to keep the man "whole." I personally find the balance sheet concept the fairest and most equitable. In addition, the policies outlined in chapters 4 and 6 should be appropriate in the relocation and administration of TCNs.

One approach being used by some companies who believe that expatriates should be allowed to maintain similar standards of living (both goods and service, and housing) in the work location have adopted a concept called the "modified balance sheet" approach. The objective behind this concept is to pay all expatriates, regardless of national origin, the same spendable portion in the work location, thus enabling them to live equally. The bottom line is different for each nationality, due to the inherent differences in nonspendable income and foreign service premium, but that portion spent in the work location is equalized. This approach is a compromise between the balance sheet and the "international cadre" approaches, but works well in places where expatriates do tend to follow similar living and housing patterns due to unavailability of alternatives.

Chapter 6

Allowances and Benefits While on Assignment

WHILE ON ASSIGNMENT ABROAD, the expatriate expects certain benefits such as assistance with the educational expenses of his children, home leave and holidays, and club memberships. He also requires aid in such unhappy instances as a death in the family. When he returns to the United States, he might expect help in acquiring housing and in capital gains tax protection. What *is* typically provided?

Educational Assistance

When an employee with dependent, school-age children is contemplating an overseas assignment, the availability and adequacy of schooling in the foreign location may determine whether or not he will accept. Obviously the decision will depend on the age of the child, the timing, the cost, and the standard of schooling in the foreign location. But basically, he has three choices: (1) he can leave his children in the care of relatives or friends, so that their present school cur-

93

riculum is uninterrupted; (2) he can take his children to the foreign location and enroll them in a suitable English-speaking (usually American subsidized) school; (3) he can put them into boarding school.

To minimize the dilemma, most companies provide an allowance for or assume the cost of securing elementary and secondary education in the foreign location. Where no English-speaking accredited schools with appropriate curricula are available in the foreign location, it is customary for companies to subsidize the cost of boarding school. The State Department defines accredited local schooling as "an educational system from which a child who completes a grade in the foreign school is able to enter the next grade in United States schools." To aid both expatriate and employer, the State Department publishes a one-page listing of foreign schools that are considered suitable for American children.

Financial assistance varies significantly between companies, and often separate policies exist for kindergarten, primary, high school, and college levels. However, I would like to suggest an approach which requires only two distinctions:

KINDERGARTEN, PRIMARY, AND SECONDARY SCHOOLING

In those instances where local public schools do not offer adequate or acceptable educational opportunities and the employee is faced with the necessity of putting his children in local private schools, a differential should be paid to meet the extra cost of providing primary (kindergarten included) and secondary schooling equivalent to public school education in the United States. The differential will normally cover actual tuition and enrollment fees, books, and transportation.

If suitable schooling is not available or acceptable in the foreign location and it is necessary to enroll children in boarding school, either inside or outside the foreign location, a differential should also be paid to cover actual transportation, room, and board. A similar differential should be paid when the child resides with relatives in the United States and attends a public school. I also recommend that where parents and children are separated as a result of schooling arrangements, the company pay for two annual roundtrip airfares between school and foreign location for the child, thus reuniting the family at regular intervals.

COLLEGE

Universally, companies pay no educational costs above the secondary school level. Expatriates whose children attend college are responsible for all tuition and other related expenses. If the child is an unmarried dependent, most companies provide one annual roundtrip airfare for the child to visit his parents in the foreign location, or, if they prefer, for one parent to return instead to the United States and visit with the child. This privilege would only be extended in those years when the expatriate family does not take home leave.

Automobile Purchase Assistance

Since most companies do not pay for the shipment of personal automobiles from the United States to the foreign location, an expatriate is forced to purchase one, or perhaps two, foreign vehicles while overseas. We have already discussed the reimbursement provision for any loss on the sale of car(s) prior to leaving the United States, but, even with this protection, the proceeds may still not be sufficient to purchase a comparable automobile in the foreign location. The cost of acquiring automobiles in some countries, such as Argentina, Malaysia or Singapore, may be prohibitive.

An expatriate should not be expected to invest excessive personal funds because a comparable automobile costs 50 to 100 percent more in the foreign location. Although it is exceedingly difficult to draft a policy which covers the purchase of such a highly discretionary commodity, most companies do offer assistance—either through financial aid, or by acquiring and providing an automobile for the expatriate's use throughout the duration of the assignment. While many companies would like to develop a uniform automobile policy, cultural and tax differences from country to country often mitigate against doing so.

My experience has been that most companies provide automobiles to very senior positions and offer some form of financial assistance to others. There is a whole variety of methods currently being utilized to determine the amount of financial aid, but one that I consider very equitable is shown in the following example and can be applied to new and used vehicles:

	Purchase Price on 1/1/78	Sale Price 2/28/80	Delta
Country of Assignment	6500	3900	2600
U.S.A.	4900	2600	2300
(per N.A.D.A. blue book)	1600[a]	1300	300[b]

This example identifies two areas that require attention: (a) the incremental purchase price of a comparable automobile, in this case $1600, and (b) the excess depreciation which the expatriate encountered, $300.

My recommendation would be to provide an interest-free loan of $1600 for the duration of the assignment, repayable net of the $300 accelerated depreciation he encountered. It is important to stipulate in your policy that vehicle purchases covered under this plan must be limited to models typically found or manufactured in the work country (e.g., VW in Germany, Fiat in Italy, Renault in France, etc.) and be medium-sized (say 1600cc), middle-priced, standard four-door sedans. Failure to be this explicit might result in your being confronted with a $30,000 request for assistance on a

Mercedes Benz 280 SL because it was the nearest thing the expatriate could find to the Corvette he sold back in the states.

Home Leave, Vacation, and Holidays

For many years expatriate employers believed it was necessary to grant lengthy home leaves to employees every two or three years, providing them with prolonged opportunities to visit families and friends in the United States, and permitting them to visit the company headquarters for briefing and orientation. It was felt that liberalness and flexibility, especially in the absence of today's rapid worldwide jet transportation, was necessary to induce qualified employees to accept foreign assignments to sometimes unpleasant and unhealthy locations. The availability of rapid air transportation and improved living conditions in many countries made lengthy home leave vacations less necessary. Companies began to recognize that the cost of assigning extra staff to cover for expatriates on lengthy home leaves and the disruption caused by their absence made it necessary to reappraise and amend their expatriate vacation policies. Expatriates themselves found that frequent, shorter vacations were more feasible and desirable.

Several companies with whom I have discussed contract length and leave provisions operate on a basis of three year assignments, with home leave after eighteen months and local leave at nine and twenty-seven months, respectively. Personally, I like this arrangement. However, four to six weeks home leave vacation taken biennially is still the most common pattern today. A number of companies still favor annual or triennial home leaves, but the majority have adopted the biennial approach. Almost universally, companies will allow home leave expenses up to the cost of direct jet economy airfare to the city in which the employee resided prior to expatriation. In addition, many companies are becoming more flexible in allowing expatriates to take home-leave vacation where they please, instead of rigidly insisting they return to the company headquarters or to the expatriate's home country, provided the cost does not exceed the roundtrip airfare mentioned above. This would allow an expatriate family in Brussels, for example, to spend four to six weeks visiting many interesting countries in Europe as opposed to returning to the States.

In designing a home leave policy, some constraints or stipulations are recommended (1) that the expatriate be made to leave the country of assignment—this is especially important where adverse climatic or other conditions make it necessary from a health standpoint; (2) that regardless of the mode of transportation selected and where he elects to spend his vacation, an expatriate be reimbursed for travel expenses not to exceed the cost of a roundtrip economy jet airfare to his home country; (3) that an expatriate not be paid cash in lieu of taking home leave; (4) that an expatriate be prohibited from accumulating leave over a number of years with the intent of taking one long, extended vacation; (5) that travel time be granted in addition to actual home leave days; and (6) that the number of days granted should not greatly exceed the total paid vacation he would have received in the States. I would suggest that three weeks vacation at home correspond to four weeks while on overseas assignment and that four weeks vacation at home correspond to five weeks while on overseas assignment.

The additional 25 or 33 percent allows time for reorientation and recovery from jet lag once the expatriate reaches his home leave destination. In all probability, this will leave him with a meaningful vacation time comparable to his peers at home.

WORK-COUNTRY VACATIONS

Local vacation policies applicable to expatriates normally follow domestic U.S. plans. Typically, vacation length is two to four weeks granted in those years where no home leave is taken—thus, if two years is the length of assignment, vacation in the work country would be taken after twelve months, and home leave at the completion of twenty-four months. Despite the fact that some expatriates would prefer to dispense with local vacations in favor of longer home leaves, it is important to make them understand that, as at home, an annual break from the job is in their best interest.

WORK-COUNTRY HOLIDAYS

The majority of companies follow local holiday practices with perhaps a few exceptions—as in Malaysia—where they are so numerous that it is impractical to do so. I would recommend that you allow expatriates at least the same number of holidays enjoyed by domestic employees, but vary the scheduling to include some key U.S. holidays (e.g., Independence Day, Thanksgiving, and Christmas), plus an appropriate number of local holidays.

COMPASSIONATE OR EMERGENCY LEAVES

The whole question of compassionate leave is so complex that I strongly recommend each case be judged on an individual basis according to its particular circumstances. As a guideline, however, most companies will, in the event of serious illness or death of a member of the employee's or spouse's immediate family, provide a roundtrip economy airfare for the employee and spouse (and children, if appropriate). Immediate family is normally considered to be spouse, children, parents, brothers, and sisters.

As I said earlier, in all cases, consideration should be given to the nature of the emergency in determining whether trips should be authorized and how much leave time permitted. As a general rule, I would advocate a two-week emergency leave be given if the employee returns to the United States, with any additional time being charged against vacation or home leave accrual.

Club Memberships

As with domestic operations, corporate policy will dictate whether an expatriate, or for that matter a local national, should join a businessman's club at company expense.

Aside from business clubs, we need to specifically address expatriate membership in sports and recreational clubs in overseas locations. My experience has been that companies seldom sponsor club memberships unless a direct business related benefit accrues to the company. We need to keep in mind, however, that man is a gregarious animal especially in strange surroundings, and those expatriates who would not normally join clubs in the United States tend to do so in foreign locations because it provides an opportunity to mix with other expatriate families. It also allows them to pursue golfing, swimming, and other social interests that might not otherwise be available to them. Public golf courses and domestic swimming pools are not common outside of the U.S., and with the exception of some European locations, continued pursuit of these recreational activities necessitates enrollment in a private club. Where possible, I would advocate that the company purchase transferable memberships to a local sports club or pay a once-only membership fee for the expatriate family. In most countries, this kind of benefit is seldom taxable and allows the expatriate executive to conduct business in congenial golf course surroundings, while his family either participates, or is not far away, enjoying the pool or tennis courts.

Termination

Whether termination of an expatriate is for cause, medical disability, or prompted by a reduction in work force, every company has an obligation to repatriate an employee to the United States. Even an expatriate who resigns prior to fulfilling his assignment has the right to a return airfare for himself and his family.

It is important, however, to note that the company's legal obligation to transport a terminated employee back to the United States may expire if that employee elects not to exercise the option before a reasonable period elapses (say one month) from the effective date of termination. Since some countries have very severe laws regarding company liability, or demand that a surety bond be posted on all expatriates at time of arrival, the legal liabilities as they pertain to both the company and the employee should be thoroughly investigated at the time the foreign service agreement is drafted.

Death of an Expatriate or Dependent While Overseas

When an employee or a member of his family dies abroad, most companies assume either the cost of local burial, or the cost of returning the body to the United States. If burial is local, reimbursable costs may include preparing the body for burial, a casket, burial plot, headstone, required documentation and fees, and any other funeral-related expenses. Where the family requests that the body be returned to the United States for burial, reimbursable costs may include preparation of the body for transportation, a shipment container, transportation costs, documentation, and any other expenses connected with the return for internment in the United States.

Some companies will reimburse the estate of the next of kin for all reasonable expenses incurred *in excess* of those which would normally occur had the death been in the United States. Either way, the expatriate should be afforded all the help possible—both financial and in kind—to minimize the trauma which, under different circumstances, would be shared by family and friends.

Repatriation Housing Allowance

An employee who sold his house prior to going abroad will most probably be confronted with a sizeable appreciation in housing prices upon repatriation. However, to my knowledge, few companies offer any type of protection to the returning expatriate—see home lease provisions covered in chapter 4.

Capital Gains Tax Protection

All expatriates who sell their principal U.S. place of residence prior to departing overseas will undoubtedly be liable for capital gains tax unless they reinvest the profits in another principal residence within four years. Since a number of "globalist" expatriates are out of the country beyond the four year transient period granted by the IRS and nearly all of them lease accommodation in the foreign location (or are provided with company-owned housing), it does present a problem for them.

To my knowledge, few companies offer any kind of reimbursement for capital gains tax, although there is a definite trend toward lease protection, thereby providing an alternative to selling.

Chapter 7
The Assignment Letter

IT IS NOT UNREASONABLE for an expatriate employer who is about to invest a considerable sum of money in an individual to try and protect his investment. Conversely, the employee needs assurance that the investment he is making in terms of loosening social ties and moving to a new environment will be adequately rewarded and that both parties are fully in agreement on the policies and procedures pertaining to his service abroad. The following is an example of a meticulous letter of assignment.

To: _____
　　　　　　(Employee's Name)
Copy: 　Payroll Department
　　　　　Employee's Personnel File
Subject: Foreign Service—Letter of Agreement
　　This letter confirms our mutual understanding of the terms and conditions applying to your international assignment. Such assignment is, of course, subject to medical

103

clearance, securing a passport, and your meeting all legal requirements for entry, work and residence in _____
_____ .

The effective date of your assignment will be the date on which you commence your journey, in accordance with company instructions, to your place of expatriate assignment. Your point of origin has been designated as _____ . The planned duration of this assignment is expected to be _____ months; any extension will be subject to mutual agreement.

Compensation

Your base salary will be $_____/month. Effective from the date of your arrival in _____ you will receive a Foreign Service Premium of $_____/month.

As soon as you move into permanent accommodation, you will receive a Living Cost Differential (LCD) to offset differences between costs in your country of assignment and the United States. Initially, your LCD will be $_____/ month. Please note that because of exchange rate fluctuations and changes in the relative cost of living between the United States and your country of assignment, your LCD will be subject to changes based on quarterly updated indices.

Additionally, if you are assigned to a location where living conditions are unusually difficult or hazardous, a Hardship Premium based on State Department indices will be paid.

You will be paid partially in the U.S. and partially in _____ (provided it is legal to operate such a split). Until such time that Payroll is advised by you to the contrary, or until changes in legislation render it illegal, your pay will be remitted _____ percent in the United States and _____ percent in _____ .

Tax Equalization

From your U.S. pay, there will be deducted an amount equivalent to the income tax you would have paid on base salary only, had you remained in the United States. Initially, your tax is $_____/month, but will be adjusted with any change in your base rate, or number of legal dependents. The company will reimburse all actual taxes you incur on company-earned income provided you utilize all legal means to minimize taxes due during your foreign assignment. The exact method of handling and accounting for your foreign tax will depend upon the specific conditions in _____ as specified by company Designated Tax Counsel (DTC).

Regardless of your actual tax burden, the company assures you that your tax liability on company earned income will be no greater than the income tax you would have paid had you not left the United States, excepting any penalties and interest levied as a result of your failure to provide the designated tax counsel with information on a timely basis. Should your actual taxes incurred be less than the amount withheld, the company will not refund the difference, the object of equalization being to ensure you neither benefit nor suffer from taxes as a result of being abroad.

Preparation and Filing of Tax Returns

In connection with the Company's tax equalization program set forth above, the Company and you further agree as follows:

1. You will comply with the tax and related laws of the United States and of any other jurisdiction authorized to impose taxes on your income, in good faith, in accordance with the interpretation of such laws furnished by company Designated Tax Counsel (DTC).
2. You will use the services of _____ (DTC) for preparation of your U.S. and any other legally required non-U.S. income tax returns, and will file, or authorize DTC to file, such returns on a timely basis.
3. The Company will pay for providing tax counsel. However, if the charges are significantly higher than for most returns because of extensive non-company items, DTC will advise you of the excess and this will be for

your account. The Company will not pay for personalized income, investment, gift, or estate planning.

4. You will furnish all information reasonably required by DTC for the preparation of your returns and will cooperate with DTC as necessary to enable DTC to prepare the returns accurately for filing on time. If you are negligent in providing DTC with the necessary information on a timely basis and, as a result, incur penalties and interest, you will be responsible for such penalties and interest.

5. You hereby authorize the Company to furnish DTC with all taxable earnings information relevant to the preparation of your return.

6. The Company will not be responsible for the accuracy of the returns prepared by DTC except in countries, if any, where local law holds the company responsible.

7. In the event DTC believes you are not complying with applicable tax laws, or are not utilizing all legal and customary means to minimize tax, you are hereby advised that DTC will notify the Company of such noncompliance.

Other Provisions of Your Assignment

1. You will receive a resettlement allowance of $_____ , payable approximately thirty days prior to departure.

2. The Company will pay a per diem of $_____/ day for up to two weeks prior to your departure for expatriate assignment should you have to vacate your home early due to selling or leasing. The Company will also pay for car rental for up to two weeks prior to your departure should you have to sell your car(s) prior to departure.

3. The Company will pay your transportation by jet economy air travel from _____ to _____ . The Company considers _____ days to be normal travel time to your country of assignment. Reimbursement for expenses while traveling to your country of assignment will be

made on submission of the appropriate expense account.

4. In addition to your allowable accompanied baggage weight, the Company will authorize the shipment of _____ pounds of personal possessions via air/sea freight. This weight allowance is applicable to both the outward and return journeys.

5. The Company will not provide for the shipment of an automobile. The Company will protect you against any loss incurred on the sale of your personal automobile(s) (one for a single person, two for a married person), reimbursing the difference between actual selling price and fair market value as indicated in the N.A.D.A. "Blue Book." Upon completion of your expatriate assignment in _____ , the Company will again protect you on loss in the sale of your personal automobile(s) (one for a single person, two for a married person), up to 25 percent of the appraised value of the car.

6. Upon arrival in _____ , the Company will pay reasonable living expenses for up to two weeks should you not be able to move directly into new quarters. If a rental car is also needed during this period, the cost will be reimbursed by the Company.

7. You agree that you will observe the work schedule in effect in your country of assignment and that you will not be entitled to overtime pay should the responsibilities of your position require you to work, from time to time, hours beyond this schedule.

8. You agree to observe the national holidays in _____ _____ , rather than those of the United States.

9. You will accrue _____ weeks of home leave, excluding travel time, upon completion of each year of your expatriate assignment commencing from your arrival date at the country of assignment. The Company will provide you and your family with round trip economy airfares _____/United States/_____ , or if you so wish, airfares to any other point outside the country of assignment provided the cost does not ex-

ceed the _____/United States/_____ round trip.

10. Through an agreement with the IRS, we are able to keep you as an active member in the Company's Pension Plan and Insurance (Health Care) Program.

11. In the event of serious illness or death of a member of your immediate family or your wife's immediate family, the Company will pay for any airfares, and grant two weeks compassionate leave, excluding travel time, so that you may return to the United States.

12. It is understood that during the term of this assignment you will not be allowed to engage in the management of, or otherwise actively pursue any business venture or any occupation that would in any way conflict with your service with, and the interests of, this Company or any affiliate of this Company, and that you will also refrain from political activity.

13. If you terminate while abroad, either at your own or the Company's option, the Company will pay all expenses to move you, your family, and your household effects back to the United States provided you return within thirty days of termination. No resettlement allowance will be paid if you voluntarily terminate or are dismissed for cause. Company initiated termination will be preceded by thirty days advance notice unless termination is for cause. If you voluntarily terminate, you are required to give a minimum of thirty days notice to the Company.

If you have any additional questions, please feel free to call or write. To confirm acceptance of these terms and conditions, and all policies set out in the Expatriate Personnel Manual, please sign below, and return one copy of this letter to the address at the front of this letter.

_____   _____
Signed (For the Company)   Signed (Employee)

_____
Date

Chapter 8

Use of the Computer in Expatriate Compensation

THE YEARS SINCE 1975 have witnessed a rapid growth in the use of computers and data processing systems in expatriate compensation. The advent of sophisticated formulas, cost-of-living indexes, hypothetical taxes, etc., that are so highly sensitive to exchange rate fluctuations, made it virtually impossible for an administrator to manually interpret, compute, and print compensation packages on a timely basis. In addition, the complexities associated with calculating compensation packages for non-U.S. expatriates gave significant impetus to the move toward computerization.

The most important thing to remember about computers is that they are not thinking machines. The computer does not make possible push-button expatriate administration in which all decisions can be made automatically. All they can do is add, subtract, multiply, divide, and compare figures in order to choose from a number of alternatives. You, the administrator, will still have to execute market-basket surveys, price housing, monitor exchange rate fluctuations, and establish tax withholding tables. However, computers will do routine and repetitive calculations at very high speeds, leaving you time to concentrate on other aspects of expatriate administration.

Below is a summary of the variables which typically affect an expatriate's compensation package and the particular items which are affected by changes in these variables. The merits of having your policy computerized becomes evident once it is realized that a typical expatriate package can conceivably change several times per year depending upon the host environment, and each change will invariably necessitate the generating of a new package.

Items Impacted

Variable	Gross Salary	ISP	Hardship	LCD	Tax	Frequency at Which Data Change
Base Salary	X	X	X	X	X	2/year
Scheduled Overtime	X			X	X	Periodically
Other Salary Premiums	X			X	X	Periodically
Home Location				X	X	Rarely
Assignment Location			X	X	X	Infrequent
Number of Tax Deductions					X	Infrequent
Number of Dependents Accompanying Expat				X	X	Infrequent
G&S COL Index				X		1-4/year
Housing Cost				X		1-2/year
Exchange Rate				X		2-6/year

In order to computerize an expatriation package, it is first necessary to have a defined compensation approach which lends itself to repetitive computations. The second condition is that all expatriate employees within a company must be covered under the same compensation policy. Some companies have a defined compensation policy but allow many employees to negotiate packages in excess of the policy amount. There will always be circumstances which warrant exceptions to the policy, but exceptions should never be allowed to become the rule. If the policy is not equitable or acceptable, change it. The third requirement is that the administrator must be able to reduce the complex computations to formulas which can be conveyed and understood by a systems analyst or computer programmer. Finally, the administrator must have access to a remote terminal or an inhouse computer system.

Programming the Computer

The real control and direction of the computer is in the hands of the human beings who use it. To carry out a particular operation, a computer must be told what to do by a set of instructions called a program. A typical program will contain hundreds of different types of instructions. Certain computational techniques, such as rounding numbers, adjusting indexes by exchange rate fluctuations, moving information from one address to another, or planning printout formats, must also be used.

The machine language which is used by the programmer and the systems techniques he utilizes are generally not the concern of an administrator. Whether the language is FORTRAN, COBAL, or some other programming language, the administrator is principally concerned with the following items and these should be conveyed to the systems analyst *before* the system is programmed to assure a flexible administrative environment.

1. The system should be operable using employee data contained on one or two eighty-column data cards. Under this approach, data changes can easily be made on the card by an administrator using a standard card punch, and also, data cards on more than one employee can be put into the system at the same time.

2. The system should have the capability to accept data input and printout packages at a remote terminal. There are times when only one or two packages are required. In situations like this, terminal input of data is more efficient than card input.

3. The system should have a memory capable of storing data used in the computations, such as cost-of-living indices, exchange rates, etc. The ability to update using video terminals is a distinct advantage.

4. The system should be capable of producing a printout of the detailed computations. Questions arise from time to time, and this capability will save time in analyzing what has changed in the expatriate's package.

5. The output format (package) should be designed to fit on one 8½ by 11 inch page, if possible. This is helpful if the form is to be filed or a copy sent to the expatriate for his records.

6. The system should be documented, not only from a programmer's standpoint, but also in such a way that administrators will have no trouble using and understanding the system.

Programming is both an art and a science which goes far beyond the scope of this book. Figure 8.1 is an example of a computerized expatriate package which was generated using hypothertical employee data.

EXPATRIATE COMPENSATION   STRICTLY PRIVATE

Concorde Company policy is to pay you, in addition to international service premium (ISP), the same after-tax salary that your work country counterpart would receive, unless your combined after-tax salary, housing and goods and services differentials amount to more.

NAME: JOHN EXPATRIATE
EMPLOYEE NUMBER: 001000
HOME COUNTRY: UNITED STATES
WORK LOCATION: MUNICH, GERMANY

Your counterpart in Munich Germany receives an annual after-tax income of 60,500 DMARK. You receive an equivalent after-tax salary of 84,912 DMARK, in addition to your international service premium. Details of your compensation are on the following pages.

PAGE 1   EXPATRIATE COMPENSATION   STRICTLY PRIVATE

Personal Information		Monthly Package			Current	
Name:	John Expatriate	Package Rate	From	1/01/81		
Employee No.	001000		To	3/31/81		Annual
H/Cntry:	United States	Base			2,500	30,000
W/Cntry:	Munich, Germany	Adjustment Before Tax	+		000	000
Base Rate	2500	G&S Fair Share (56.5)	−		1,413	16,956
Percent of U.S. Midpoint	95	Housing Share (23.7)	−		593	7,119
Job Grade	20	Hypothetical Tax	−		392	4,700
Martial Status	M	Disposable Income =	+		102	1,225
Number of Exemptions	4	ISP	+		375	4,500
Family Size at Loc	4	Non-Stnd Hardship	+		000	000
		Resident Hardship	+		000	000
		Adjustment After Tax	+		000	000
		Payable in US Dollars	+		478	5,731

Work Location/				
Base X Exch. Rate X 80.2			4,010	48,120
G&S Different. (Index = .50)		+	1,413	16,956
Housing Differential		+	696	8,352
Position Allowance		+	000	000
Payable In	DMARK	=	6,120	73,450

PAGE 2   EXPATRIATE COMPENSATION   STRICTLY PRIVATE

CALCULATION OF MONTHLY PACKAGE

(ANNUAL = MONTHLY x 12)

	Home Country:	United States
Effective Date 1/01/81	Work Location:	Munich, Germany

Goods And Services Differential (G&S):

1. Adjusted G&S Index	=	G&S Index	X	Survey Exch. Rate	/	Exch. Rate
	1.500	=	1.500	X	2.0	/	2.0
2. G&S Factor	=	Adjusted G&S Index −	1			
	.500	=	1.500 −	1			
3. G&S Fair Share	=	Base Rate	X	Spendable Income %		
U.S. Dollars	1,413	=	U.S.Dollars 2,500	=	56.5		
4. G&S Differential	=	G&S Fair Share	X	G&S Factor X	Exch. Rate	
DMARK	1,413	=	U.S. Dollars 1,413	X	.500 X	2.0	

Housing Differential:

1. H/C Housing Cost Est.	=	Base Salary	X	H/C Housing Cost %	
U.S. Dollars	593	=	U.S. Dollars 2,500	X	23.7	
2. Differential	=	W/C Housing Cost	−	H/C Housing Est. X Exch. Rate	
DMARK	696	=	DMARK 1883	−	(593 X 2.0)	

PAGE 3   EXPATRIATE COMPENSATION   STRICTLY PRIVATE

EFFECTIVE 1/01/81 IN MUNICH, GERMANY

Currency:	U.S. Dollars		Monthly		Yearly
	Base Rate		2,500		30,000
	Adjustment Before Tax	+	000	+	000
	Salary Allowance	+	000	+	000
	Hypothetical Tax	−	392	−	4,700
	International Service Premium (ISP)	+	375	+	4,500
	Living Cost Differential	+	1,054	+	12,656
	Resident Hardship Premium	+	000	+	000
	Non-Standard Hardship Premium	+	000	+	000
	Adjustment After Tax	+	000	+	000
	= Total Compensation		3,537		42,456

			**** Salary ****		
Recmnd. Salary Split	U.S. Dollars/Mo. Exch. Rate	Monthly	Yearly	Currency
H/Cntry: United States	619 X 1.00	478	5,731	U.S. Dollars
W/Loctn: Munich, Germany	3060 X 2.00	6120	73,450	DMARK

113

Chapter 9

Expatriate Cost Models

The cost of managing an international business is already greater than a domestic business. Investment stakes are high and mistakes are costly—so are expatriates.

—Stan Frith

IT NEVER CEASES to amaze me how minimal is the attention paid by many large corporations to the bottom line cost, both financial and people-resource, of maintaining an expatriate overseas. Management occasionally looks at the total cost, but invariably they focus their attention solely on the remunerative aspect of expatriation expense. In most cases, this represents less than half the incremental cost of placing and maintaining an expatriate overseas.

In reality, there is no substitute for having well-trained local nationals in key managerial positions in overseas operations. If they are of the right caliber, they understand the local business environment and will have well-established ties with senior businessmen and government officials. They can infiltrate bureaucracies, cut red tape, and add an element of continuity that is lost when expatriates are used. This places the company in a more favorable light with local government agencies, other nationally owned companies, and the local work force, whom they must direct and motivate and to whom they must relate; it is also far more cost effective and offers a long-term investment as opposed to the short-term solution of using expatriates. The most successful multinational corporations that I have had dealings with prefer to bring qualified local nationals to the United States for a year, train them in the company's managerial philosophy, and send them back as plant managers, controllers, personnel directors, etc. For the more technical or engineering roles or where many nationals need to be trained, obviously it may be justified to send an expatriate to train them as opposed to bringing them all to the states.

It has been my observation that the product-line manager who sanctions the utilization of an American or third country national for an international assignment is concerned primarily with accomplishing a specific goal within a short time period, and unless it is called to his attention, minimal consideration is given to the cost. In the majority of cases, cost *should* be secondary when an urgent task has to be performed overseas and there is nobody qualified to handle it locally. However, there are a substantial number of expatriates overseas whose contributions do not justify their expense. These lower-level and middle-level employees would probably not have been sent, had the manager been supplied with an estimate of the relative cost compared to hiring and training a local national. If you consider that it could cost in excess of $200,000 per year to expatriate an American executive and his family to Japan as opposed to around $60,000 per year to hire an executive level Japanese national, you can see how a poor decision would affect local profits.

As management becomes increasingly aware of the cost trade-offs associated with sending domestic employees abroad, the expatriate administrator will be requested to furnish more and more supportive material for them to review. The only problem is that the knowledge and availability of data for calculating the true cost of maintaining an international employee is beyond the scope of all but a few personnel administrators. In order to forecast ahead of time the total cost of expatriation, it is often necessary to design a data base capable of assimilating a matrix of variable costs both indigenous and foreign, perform a multitude of relatively complex tax calculations, and accurately select those costs, both internal and external, that might conceivably affect a particular employee under a given set of circumstances.

Estimating Expatriate Costs

Quantifying and communicating expatriate costs is generally achieved by the development of a cost model which itemizes all the expense items associated with the employee's assignment. An examination of most expatriate policies reveals that, in addition to the cost factors usually documented in the expatriate's compensation package, there are between fifteen and twenty peripheral reimbursements or allowances paid to an expatriate in the course of an assignment. These allowances and reimbursable items range from relocation expenses normally paid by the company, to exchange-rate protection provisions which are gaining a limited acceptance.

The key to effectively utilizing a cost model is to keep the approach simple and straightforward. There is a tendency to overcomplicate the cost model concept by laboriously attempting to collect precise and unique cost data for each employee, rather than utilizing reasonable assumptions which will suffice for a variety of assignment variables. For instance, the cost of educating children overseas in private schools can vary from work country to work country. An alternative to diligently keeping exact records of educational costs in each country is to assume a median cost and update the estimate annually. This functional approach is never too far off and allows an administrator to concentrate his attention on the high cost items such as the compensation package and tax reimbursement.

Figure 9.1 is an example of a cost estimate which would be meaningful to a manager evaluating the profit and loss impact of sending an expatriate to Germany for a two year assignment. It is made up of actual costs where readily available and reasonable estimates where appropriate.

Fig. 9.1

Data Input to Model

1. Length of Assignment — Two years
2. Home Country — United States
3. Work Country — Germany
4. Family Status — Married, two children (ages 8, 12)
5. Base Salary — $30,000 per year
6. Other — Data required to generate compensation package
   — Specific provisions of expatriate relocation policy

Model Output

Expatriate Cost Estimate—Concord Industries

Employee Name: John Expatriate
Home Country: United States　　Work Country: Germany
Assignment: Manufacturing Superintendent

Compensation Package

	Cost for 2 Year Assignment
Base Salary	$60,000
International Service Premium	9,000
Living Cost Differential	25,312
Hypothetical Tax Withholding	(9,400)
Subtotal	84,912

Transfer to Work Country

Relocation Allowance (2 months salary)	5,000
Home Sale/Lease Protection (Brokers Fee)	5,250

Auto Sale Protection (2 cars)	700
Departure Expenses (2 weeks motel)	850
Furniture Storage	1,100
Personal Goods Shipment (1400 lbs)	2,800
Car Rental (2 weeks)	250
Airfare (Economy Class)	2,400
Subtotal	18,350

Work Country Expenses

Arrival Expenses (1 Month Hotel)	2,250
Home Leave (Round Trip Airfare)	4,800
Language Lessons (Employee and Spouse)	3,000
Educational Allowance (Two Children)	5,400
Tax Equalization Costs	54,600
Tax Services	1,800
Departure Expenses (1 Week Hotel)	500
Car Rental (3 Weeks)	380
Subtotal	72,730

Transfer to Home Country

Relocation Allowance (1 Months Salary)	2,500
Auto Sale Protection (2 cars)	700
Arrival Expenses (2 weeks motel)	850
Personal Goods Shipment	2,800
Airfare (Economy Class)	2,400
Car Rental (2 weeks)	250
Subtotal	9,500
Total Estimated Expatriate Cost for 2-Year Assignment:	185,492

Expatriate Cost Analysis

Cost to utilize expatriate	$92,746/yr
Cost of comparable local national	$40,750/yr
Cost premium of utilizing expatriate	$51,996/yr
Expatriate Cost as percentage of Employee's Base Salary	309
Expatriate Cost as percentage of Base Salary of Local National	228

Conclusion

As one can readily see, many of the variable expenses in an expatriate cost model are derived as a function of some other employee statistic such as base salary, family size, etc. This relationship lends itself to computerization. While many administrators still do cost estimating manually, the problems they face are numerous; poor cycle time, a high rate of errors, and a significant drain on professional and clerical labor are only a few. I therefore believe the computerized cost model is a logical extension of a computerized compensation package. A cost summary can be generated automatically each time a new package is calculated. This would facilitate not only a cost review before an employee becomes an expatriate, but also allow the costs of an expatriate on assignment to be monitored and accurately forecasted for planning purposes on an ongoing basis. In addition, the truly complex portion of the cost model—the tax equalization calculations—could be done quickly and accurately.

Chapter 10

Communication

While good communications are no substitute for sound policies, responsible attitudes, and mutual confidence, good communication can prevent these assets from being undermined by misunderstanding and lack of information.
—Stan Frith

IF YOU THINK it is hard to successfully administer and communicate personnel policies and compensation practices within North America, where there is just one currency and a single, reasonably stable inflation rate, wait until you start administering expatriates; and, if you really want to set yourself a challenge, add a number of third country nationals to the payroll. In the United States, we at least have uniformity of language, currency, education, inflation, and the relative homogeneity of culture and ideology, but for expatriates or third country nationals we may have none of those factors. Because of the highly individualistic and complex parameters and variables that affect an expatriate's compensation and way of life, communicating with him can impose problems for even the most seasoned professional personnel administrator.

As we have seen in earlier chapters, as the personnel representative in charge of expatriate administration, you devote considerable time to selecting and orientating these individuals prior to sending them abroad. Don't now nullify all that good work by simply ignoring them after they board the airplane. Regrettably, and in many cases quite justifiably, this is how many expatriates perceive the situation. The old adage, "Out of sight, out of mind," is their constant war cry and, unfortunately, where there truly is a lack of definitive communication, they have every right to be dissident.

Continual perturbations in inflation rates and resulting currency fluctuations can create havoc with an expatriate compensation package. Even the most sophisticated and intricate compensation program that is both equitable within the organization and competitive with that provided by other employers in the industry can still generate animosity if communication and understanding are not implicit. Feedback channels must be kept open in order to constantly review unique problems, stop rumors, and correct misunderstandings or unintentional errors. If a company aims to get a viable return from the investment of sending an expatriate overseas, the expatriate must function effectively. This task is already made difficult by the environmental, language, and cultural differences under which he must operate. If he is also having to contend with fears about the sustainability of the compensation package, his effectiveness must be virtually zero. Just like any domestic operation, once the expatriate policies and compensation programs have been established and are operating, expatriates should be reminded periodically of their existence and objectives. There are a number of ways to communicate this kind of information:

● Have one-on-one discussions prior to departure and each time the expatriate visits the United States or when you, the administrator, visit the overseas location.
● Make periodic presentations to groups of expatriates.

- Distribute handbooks which spell out the objectives and mechanics of the expatriate package in detail.
- Periodically send out literature or articles that address expatriate policies, problems, or general information.

It is almost an axiom that expatriates must be kept informed; communicating information not only about pay, but about future plans you have for the expatriate, is not only important, but vitally necessary. Well-informed expatriates, like any other employees, feel a sense of participation and belonging. Suggestions come readily from them. Where lines of personnel policy are clearly defined and the areas of uncertainty and speculation are reduced, few will be tempted to a breach of the policy. Where standards are clearly established, the flexibility needed to meet changing conditions can be introduced without arousing the feeling among expatriates that sheer caprice governs policy.

Success in imparting information to expatriates on the sustainability of the compensation package, benefits, and general policy and procedures is linked closely with the extent to which they feel involved in the success of the business and in the reality of the company's expressed interest in them. Confidence and trust can neither be bought cheaply nor hurriedly pumped into the organization. Like anybody else, expatriates are interested in conditions of employment, methods of payment, the opportunities that exist for them on repatriation (in terms of further training and promotion), and the general well-being of the corporation. The quality of management in ensuring good communication will determine whether this interest is nurtured or dissipated.

Chapter 11

A Few Words to the Expatriate

Travel, in the younger sort, is part of education; in the older, a part of experience.

—Francis Bacon

HAVE YOU EVER VISITED one of our major international airports and heard someone announce a departure, say, to Geneva, and immediately you envision tranquil and serene Swiss lakes and alps shimmering hazily in the distance? Or perhaps the flight was to Venice where buildings that house some of the greatest works of art in Europe are separated by narrow canals on which gondolas and light motor launches operate as taxis or buses. Or, maybe the unseen voice at the airport addressed passengers to Rio de Janeiro and, unwittingly, a picture of Copacabana beach and Sugarloaf mountain last seen on an old office calendar was mentally reproduced. Just for a second, the urge to travel clutched your mind, and the desire to seek new, perhaps permanent, horizons on richer continents than ours registered—then, as quickly, dissolved.

Not all roads lead to Rome. In England it often rains when it isn't foggy, and, in Kuwait, temperatures do reach 120 degrees while sixty mile per hour sandstorms are not uncommon. But, for those Americans who might be enchanted by another country's history, monuments, art galleries, museums, archaeological discoveries, wildlife, beaches, and even food, an expatriate assignment is a unique opportunity to consummate those dreams while sharing and living another culture.

Sound interesting? It will be interesting, but it won't be easy. There is definitely no room internationally for Americans who are failures at home, who are neophobiacs, or who simply seek to escape from an irreconcilable domestic situation. Unless you and your family are adaptable and unprovincial, with a genuine free spirit and a desire to go abroad, do not waste your time or the company's money. You really must be willing to loosen old social ties and adapt to new cultural and social norms; you will have to overcome language barriers and climatic, political and even religious differences. Still interested? Then read on.

The Checklist

Once you have signed on the dotted line and discussed and agreed upon the terms and conditions of the transfer, it is important that you immediately begin to prepare yourself. Remember, the more you do now, the better equipped you will be to handle the adjustment when the time comes. The following checklist should help.

☐ Insist that your personnel manager set up an appointment for an orientation and briefing session as soon as possible, and preferably before you start to make arrangements to sell your house and car or to ship furniture, etc. Be sure that you are fully conversant with company policy before proceeding any further.

☐ Read and learn as much about the country of assignment as you possibly can. Visit your local library or call the host country's embassy here in the United States and ask them to mail you any literature they may have. Collect as much information as you can about the country, people, culture, politics, climate, medical facilities, schooling, housing, shopping, and tax and labor laws. Write to other expatriates already in the foreign location or to the U.S. embassy in the country and ask them for information.

☐ Be sure you are fully briefed on and understand the objectives and job-related responsibilities associated with the assignment.

☐ If you have been assigned to a country in which the local language is alien to you, it is imperative that you begin language training. Acquire at least a working knowledge of the language before you leave.

☐ Disposal of your home should be of primary consideration. Will you sell or rent? If the latter, will you rent furnished or unfurnished? If your company operates a home-sale or lease protection program, familiarize yourself with it, and work toward reaching an early decision. Consult a real estate agent, and, whether your decision is to sell or lease, get the agent working on it. Discuss the provisions of the capital gains tax laws with a CPA before making the final decision to sell.

☐ Advertise your automobile(s). Once sold, cancel your automobile insurance and inquire if a refund is due. Notify the Department of Motor Vehicles of the ownership change.

☐ Make sure each family member has a valid passport and that the necessary visas and work permits have been acquired.

☐ Get a thorough medical, dental, and optical checkup. Be certain that you have received all the necessary vaccinations and inoculations required for work in the host country. The U.S. Public Health Service can advise you on this.

☐ Contact a moving company. Most reputable moving companies also provide a packing service for a slightly higher fee.

☐ Contact a storage company.

☐ If you don't already have a will, consult your attorney and have one drawn up.

☐ Check with your insurance agent to see if they need additional information to extend coverage while you are overseas.

☐ At least four weeks before departure date, go through the entire house and garage identifying items to be shipped, those to be stored, and those that can be discarded. Now is an excellent time to conduct a garage sale or to donate things to a local charity.

☐ Notify the following of your move overseas, and where necessary, supply them with the company's overseas address. Many expatriates continue to have all mail directed to the company post office box because of the sometimes unreliable foreign postal services.

☐ Accountant
☐ Bank
☐ Book/Record Clubs
☐ Church or Temple
☐ Credit Card Companies*
☐ Country Club
☐ Dentist
☐ Doctor
☐ Federal/State Tax Bureaus
☐ Finance Company
☐ Fraternity
☐ Friends
☐ Insurance Agencies
☐ Lawyer
☐ Optician
☐ Relatives
☐ Schools/Colleges
☐ Social Security Office
☐ Sorority
☐ Stockbroker
☐ Your landlord (if you are a tenant)
☐ Your tenants (if you are a landlord)

---

*Do not cancel credit cards, as you will need them when you return to the United States. Simply contact each company and advise them of your temporary relocation overseas.

☐ Cancel the following:

    ☐ Newspapers   ☐ Club Memberships

    ☐ Magazines   ☐ Auto Insurance

☐ Arrange for disconnection of the following:

    ☐ Telephones   ☐ Utilities

☐ Open up a document file, keep it in a safe place, and make sure it contains copies of:

    ☐ Birth Certificates   ☐ Bank Books

    ☐ Marriage Certificate   ☐ Wills

    ☐ School Records   ☐ Portfolio Records

    ☐ Insurance Policies   ☐ Expense Receipts (either

    ☐ Medical Records   for reimbursement from the

    ☐ Vaccination   company or to include with

       Certificates   your tax return)

    ☐ Dental Records   ☐ Prior Year Tax Records

    ☐ Driver's License   ☐ Photographs (for exit/

    ☐ Police Clearance   re-entry visas, permit

                      renewals, etc.)

☐ Prepare your pet(s) for relocation in conjunction with advice for your local veterinarian.

☐ Plan food purchases so that on the day you leave, the pantry will be empty.

A Word about Moving

Having checked off everything on the above list, the only major item still to be accomplished is moving. In the absence of forethought, packaging and moving household goods can be chaotic. But, given a little organization, order and harmony can prevail. To assist the mover and packers, the following checklist may prove useful.

BEFORE MOVERS ARRIVE

☐ Place marker tags on all items you do not want packed. Or better still, move them into a separate room and notify the packers accordingly.

☐ Clearly identify those items to be shipped and those to be stored, since different packaging material may be required. Also, it is very embarrassing to discover, after everything is packaged and is no longer easily recognizable, that you forgot to separate the two and are forced to tear open the corners of packages to see what's inside and where it is to go.

☐ Have all crockery and cutlery washed, dried, and in the cabinets.

☐ Leave beds assembled, but with bedclothes removed.

☐ Make sure all bed linens, towels, etc., are washed, dried, and left in the cupboards.

WHEN MOVERS ARRIVE

☐ Make sure you are on hand, at the prearranged time, to receive them.

☐ Accompany them on a tour of the house, pointing out which items are for shipment, which for storage, and which items should be packed. They will inspect and tag each piece of furniture with an identifying number. These numbers, along with a description of the goods and the condition they are in, will appear on the inventory.

☐ Point out fragile, valuable, or antique items that will require special packaging and handling.

☐ Keep out of the way, but be close enough to answer any questions they may have.

BEFORE MOVERS LEAVE

☐ Make a last tour of the premises to be certain they have not overlooked anything or that something got packed you wanted left behind.

☐ Thoroughly check the inventory, then sign it. Make sure you retain a copy for yourself.

☐ Sign the combination bill of lading and freight bill which states the terms and conditions under which your goods are being moved. Read the small print to avoid legal entanglements later. A copy should be retained as your receipt.

☐ Make certain the bill of lading bears the correct amount for declared valuation protection. If you require alternative coverage, make sure you specify, in your own handwriting, the coverage plan you desire.

☐ Verify that the mover has the exact destination addresses —the storage company and the overseas address—plus an address where you can be contacted in case of an emergency.

It's Time to Go

Most companies endeavor to avoid last minute hassles by encouraging prospective expatriates to sell their automobiles and vacate their residence at least one week prior to their departure date. In return, they reimburse the cost of a leased vehicle and transient accommodation. Whether headed for a motel or the airport, be sure to check around the house one last time. Be sure that:

☐ All windows are shut and locked.

☐ Safety poles are wedged inside all exterior sliding glass doors.

☐ Water is shut off and all pipes are drained.

☐ Furnace and air conditioner are shut off.

☐ Utilities are disconnected.

☐ Lights are turned off.

☐ Front and rear doors are locked.

☐ Neighbors are notified and provided with a key.

☐ Police are notified if house is to remain vacant for any length of time.

☐ Somebody has been assigned to maintain the yard and/or pool.

☐ Tenants or new owner have been advised of vacant status.

A Word about Passports

Passports are issued by the Department of State through its offices in leading cities. A nominal fee is charged, and they are valid for five years unless limited to a shorter period by the secretary of state. Your passport is the most important identification document and proof of citizenship you have. It grants you authority to leave the United States and requests that the country or countries of destination allow you entry. Keep it in your possession at all times when traveling, and store it in a safe place when not. (Copies of Department of State publication form DSP-11 are included at the end of this chapter.)

A Word about Travelers' Checks

Travelers' checks were developed in 1891 by Marcellus Berry, and since that time, have served a useful role in international travel. The primary purpose of these checks is to eliminate the need for travelers to carry large sums of cash that could easily get lost or stolen. The checks are made out by travel agents or banks and are redeemable almost anywhere in the United States and in most countries of the world. A slight fee is charged for their issuance, but it is a small price to pay for the protection afforded by this type of money order. I strongly recommend that if you are going to incur expenses en route, you purchase travelers' checks and not carry large amounts of cash.

A Word about the Journey

Your company will probably insist that their staff travel by the most direct route on economy jet air transportation. I think that's fine. With today's wide-based aircraft, it is conceivable that those lucky devils with "XYZ Company" are more cramped traveling first class than you and your family will be stretched out across several seats in the economy section. On very long flights, your company will encourage you to break the journey and spend a day or so at a convenient place en route. One alternative to this (and one that I think is a better arrangement) is to proceed without any break and take the time off on arrival in the new location. While recuperating from jet lag and the exhaustion of being confined for a long time in an airplane, you can relax and take a leisurely look at your new location. From my own experience, stopping off somewhere for one or two days, especially with the family in tow, is contrary to reason. There is insufficient time to see anything worthwhile, and by the time you have cleared customs, hassled with taxi drivers, paid exorbitant prices for hotels (we all tend to stop over in the more popular, tourist cities), struggled with bags, and perhaps almost missed the onward flight due to some unforeseen problem, you may be more exhausted than if you had continued nonstop.

Some do's connected with the flight:
- If there are certain foods you cannot eat because of dietetic or religious reasons, notify the airline both at the time of making reservations and a few days before departure date.
- If you have a history of motion sickness problems, get the company physician or your doctor to prescribe some medication.
- Arrange for the taxi a day ahead of time.
- Call the airport before setting out to make sure the flight is not unduly delayed.
- Arrive at the airport at least forty-five minutes before domestic departures and one hour and a quarter before international flights (unless otherwise stated).
- Hold carry-on baggage to a minimum.
- While most airlines provide magazines for adults, coloring books and games for children, and an assortment of candies, it never hurts to bring along a few favorite books or puzzles to help while away the hours.

- If you have any kind of problem or discomfort during the flight, notify the cabin staff immediately. They are trained to handle most emergency situations and would prefer that you have them chase down medication than clean up after a bout of upset stomach.

Upon Arrival

Presumably the company will have somebody at the airport to meet you. I suggest you go straight to a hotel and rest for at least twenty-four hours. There is medical evidence to support the belief that anyone suffering from travel fatigue who goes immediately to work is prone to make mistakes and wrong decisions.

Once you are rested, visit your office and inquire about the availability of a car and what arrangements have been made for house hunting. Although the company will grant full living expenses until regular housing is available and your furniture arrives, the sooner you start looking, the better. Unless there are real work-related pressures that demand your immediate involvement in business matters, take a week to view houses and perhaps purchase a car. The alternative is plenty of fragmented effort and distraction. If you really cannot afford the time, arrange for your spouse to be given a tour and select living quarters. Before signing any contract, make sure you review the following—

- Location of schools and school bus routes
- Distance from the office
- Whereabouts of existing expatriate communities
- Location of shopping facilities
- Location of sports and social clubs and churches or temples
- Cost of apartments versus housing
- Rents in the suburbs versus downtown

If you are moving directly into company-owned housing, the

above may not be pertinent. But, if you are not, consider all of the above before signing a lease. Make certain you fully understand the contract and that it contains a provision for early termination in the event you are transferred again before expiration of the lease. Normal penalty for early termination under these circumstances is one month's rent in lieu of notice; but, if the provision is not included and you terminate six months before the agreement is scheduled to expire, the landlord may be entitled to six months' rent.

When purchasing a car, limit your search to models typically found or manufactured in the host country. The reasons are the same as for buying an American car in the United States—price, availability of service and spare parts, design (built to suit local roads and traffic conditions), economics (price of gasoline), and resale value. Where language might be a barrier in negotiating the purchase price, take a reliable member of the local staff with you. Make sure that you comply with local regulations with regard to change of ownership, registration, and taxes. Also, be sure that your U.S. driver's license is sufficient for you to commence driving. Some countries require you to take a test locally, but it is usually fairly basic and should present no problems.

There really isn't much more that I can help you with, except perhaps to remind you of something James Conant, one-time U.S. Ambassador to West Germany, was quoted as saying: "Behavior which appears superficially correct, but is intrinsically corrupt, always irritates those who see below the surface."

I will close this chapter by listing a few of the do's and don't's that we should observe. We have a habit of forgetting some of these once we leave the United States and become frustrated by unusual customs and indigenous governments, service industries, and life-styles. Remember, we are all ambassadors of the United States, and people in foreign lands will tend to judge our whole nation by the way we perform and conduct ourselves in their country.

• Avoid using derogatory remarks about the local people or their country, even if you know they cannot understand you. It is easy to fall into this trap, especially when in the company of other Americans. Remember, few nationalities share the so-called American sense of humor or our ability to accept ridicule or criticism from strangers. So don't be careful—*don't do it!*

• American directness is not universal. Many cultures favor the opposite approach which avoids confrontation. Instead of telling it like it is, they tell it like they think you want it to be. You may find this frustrating, but be patient.

• The American way isn't everybody's way, and foreign nationals will soon resent statements that begin "back home we do . . ." or "in the states we have . . . ." An exasperated host may suggest that you return home if you miss it so much.

• Seemingly endless red tape, paperwork, bureaucracies, interruptions, strikes, siestas, and general work delays will try the patience of most time-oriented Americans. Don't lose your cool.

• Most Americans are used to automation, high speed, and efficiency—instant everything. Be prepared for a lack of these conveniences and, even worse, lack of regular conveniences such as heat, air conditioning, drinkable water, television, and English newspapers and magazines.

• Supercilious, pretentious, egotistical, and insensitive—I have heard all these criticisms and many more leveled at Americans living abroad. Try to keep a low profile and exercise restraint—"Act like an American" is about the worst advice you can give to some people!

• The dollar is our unit of currency, and we are proud of it. Well, citizens of other countries are proud of theirs. The denomination or the shape of the coins may seem irregular to us, but that does not justify discourteous references to "funny money" or "toy money." Show the same respect for their currency as you would expect them to show for the dollar.

● If the company was considerate enough to sponsor language training, try not to be self-conscious—give it a try. You will often find the local people are far more cooperative and friendly when they detect some effort on your part to integrate by communicating with them in their native tongue.

● Be gastronomically adventuresome and try local dishes when eating out. There's nothing worse than overhearing an American order hamburger and fries in a reputable local restaurant renowned for its antipasto, Bratwurst, or *canard sauvage*. The same goes for wines; how else will you be able to recommend a good Chianti, Madeira or *vin du pays* to your friends back home?

A

DEPARTMENT OF STATE
PASSPORT APPLICATION

TO BE TYPED OR PRINTED IN INK BY ALL APPLICANTS

(First name)   (Middle name)   (Last name)

I, _____
a citizen of the United States, do hereby apply to the Department of State for a passport.

MAIL PASSPORT TO:
IN CARE OF (If applicable): _____
STREET _____
CITY _____ STATE _____ ZIP CODE _____
PHONE NO. Area Code: _____ Home: _____ Business: _____

SEX	BIRTHPLACE (City, State or Province, Country)	BIRTH DATE Month Day Year
☐ Male ☐ Female		

DEPARTURE DATE	HEIGHT ___ Ft. ___ In.	COLOR OF HAIR	COLOR OF EYES

PERMANENT RESIDENCE (Street address, City, State, ZIP Code) | SOCIAL SECURITY NO. (Not mandatory)

(PASSPORT OFFICE USE ONLY)
R D O DP Endorsement_____

APPLICANT'S EVIDENCE OF CITIZENSHIP

☐ Birth Certificate   SR   CR   City
☐ Certificate of Naturalization or Citizenship
☐ Passport
Bearer's Name:
No.:   Filed/Issued:
Place: ☐ Seen & Returned

2" X 2"   FROM 1" TO 1-3/8"

FOR DETAILED PHOTOGRAPH REQUIREMENTS, SEE ATTACHED INFORMATION SHEET. ACCEPTANCE AGENT WILL STAPLE PHOTO OF BEARER HERE.

FATHER'S NAME	BIRTHPLACE	BIRTH DATE	U.S. CITIZEN ☐ Yes ☐ No
MOTHER'S MAIDEN NAME	BIRTHPLACE	BIRTH DATE	U.S. CITIZEN ☐ Yes ☐ No

☐ I WAS LAST MARRIED ON _____ TO (Wife's/Husband's full legal/maiden name - complete whether married, widowed or divorced)
☐ I WAS NEVER MARRIED

HAVE YOU OR ANYONE TO BE INCLUDED IN YOUR PASSPORT (SEE SECTION B BELOW) EVER BEEN ISSUED OR INCLUDED IN A U.S. PASSPORT?   ☐ Yes ☐ No
IF YES, SUBMIT PASSPORT. IF UNABLE TO SUBMIT MOST RECENT PASSPORT, STATE ITS DISPOSITION: NO.:   ISSUE DATE:

IN THE EVENT OF ACCIDENT OR DEATH NOTIFY (Not mandatory) (Do not give name of person who will accompany you when traveling)
Name in full: Relationship:
Address: Phone No.:

B

ACCEPTANCE AGENT WILL STAPLE PHOTO OF PERSON(S) HERE.

AGENT SHALL NOT IMPRESS SEAL ON ANY PHOTOGRAPHS.

PHOTO REQUIREMENTS FOR PERSON(S) TO BE INCLUDED
See detailed photograph requirements on the attached information sheet.
Photo must be ONLY of person(s) to be included (other than passport bearer). When more than one person is to be included, a group photo of the inclusions is required.

COMPLETE IF CHILDREN OR BROTHERS AND SISTERS UNDER AGE 13, AND/OR WIFE/HUSBAND, ARE TO BE INCLUDED AND SUBMIT PHOTO

WIFE'S/HUSBAND'S FULL LEGAL NAME

BIRTHPLACE (City, State or Province, Country)	BIRTH DATE (Mo., Day, Yr.)

CHILD(REN)'S NAME(S) IN FULL	BIRTHPLACE(S) (City, State or Country)	BIRTHDATE(S) (Mo., Day, Yr.)

(PASSPORT OFFICE USE ONLY)
WIFE'S/HUSBAND'S EVIDENCE

☐ Seen & Returned

CHILD(REN)'S EVIDENCE

☐ Seen & Returned

I have not (and no other person included in this application has), since acquiring United States citizenship, performed any of the acts listed in section I on the reverse of this application form (unless explanatory statement is attached). I solemnly swear (or affirm) that the statements made on all of the pages of this application are true and the photograph(s) attached is (are) a likeness of me and of those persons to be included in the passport.

_____ (SEAL) _____
(To be signed at same time by husband/wife to be included in passport)   (To be signed by applicant in presence of person administering oath)

Subscribed and sworn to (affirmed) before me this _____ day of _____ 19 _____ .

Clerk of the _____, Postal Employee/Passport Agent at _____
                                          (Signature of person authorized to accept application)

(PASSPORT OFFICE USE ONLY)

FEE _____ EXEC. _____ POST. _____

FORM DSP-11
7-79

(OVER – YOU MUST COMPLETE PAGE 2)

FORM APPROVED
OMB NO. 47–R0051

138

C

TO BE COMPLETED BY ALL APPLICANTS		
OCCUPATION	VISIBLE DISTINGUISHING MARKS	COUNTY OF RESIDENCE (Not mandatory)

D

APPLICANTS MUST COMPLETE FOLLOWING IF MARRIED, WIDOWED OR DIVORCED		
WIFE'S/HUSBAND'S BIRTH PLACE	WIFE'S/HUSBAND'S BIRTH DATE	U.S. CITIZEN ☐ Yes ☐ No	☐ MARRIAGE NOT TERMINATED ☐ MARRIAGE TERMINATED BY ☐ DEATH ☐ DIVORCE ON (Date) _____

E

WOMEN MUST COMPLETE FOLLOWING IF CHILDREN OF A PREVIOUS MARRIAGE ARE INCLUDED OR IF PREVIOUSLY MARRIED BEFORE MARCH 3, 1931

I WAS PREVIOUSLY MARRIED ON	TO (Full legal name)	WHO WAS BORN AT (City, State, Country)
ON (Date of birth)	☐ FORMER HUSBAND WAS U.S. CITIZEN ☐ FORMER HUSBAND WAS NOT U.S. CITIZEN	PREVIOUS MARRIAGE TERMINATED BY ☐ DEATH ☐ DIVORCE ON (Date) _____

F

COMPLETE IF APPLICANT OR ANY PERSON INCLUDED IN SECTION B WAS NOT BORN IN THE UNITED STATES AND CLAIMS CITIZENSHIP THROUGH PARENT(S)

ENTERED THE U.S. (Month) (Year) ☐ Applicant ☐ Wife ☐ Husband ☐ Child	IF FATHER NATURALIZED:		IF KNOWN, FATHER'S RESIDENCE/PHYSICAL PRESENCE IN U.S. From (Year) To (Year)
	Date	Certificate No.	
	Before (Name of Court)	Place (City, State)	
RESIDENCE/CONTINUOUS PHYSICAL PRESENCE IN U.S. From (Year) To (Year) ☐ Applicant ☐ Wife ☐ Husband ☐ Child	IF MOTHER NATURALIZED:		IF KNOWN, MOTHER'S RESIDENCE/PHYSICAL PRESENCE IN U.S. From (Year) To (Year)
	Date	Certificate No.	
	Before (Name of Court)	Place (City, State)	

G

PROPOSED TRAVEL PLANS (For statistical reporting purposes—Not Mandatory)		
PURPOSE OF TRIP	MEANS OF TRANSPORTATION Ship Air Other	COUNTRIES TO BE VISITED
	Departure ☐ ☐ ☐	
PROPOSED LENGTH OF STAY	Return ☐ ☐ ☐	
NO. OF PREVIOUS TRIPS ABROAD WITHIN LAST 12 MONTHS	DO YOU EXPECT TO TAKE ANOTHER TRIP ABROAD? ☐ Yes ☐ No IF SO WITHIN ☐ 1 Year ☐ 2 Years ☐ 5 Years	

H

PRIVACY ACT STATEMENT

The information solicited on this form is authorized by, but not limited to, those statutes codified in Titles 8, 18, and 22, United States Code, and all predecessor statutes whether or not codified, and all regulations issued pursuant to Executive Order 11295 of August 5, 1966. The primary purpose for soliciting the information is to establish citizenship, identity and entitlement to issuance of a United States Passport or related facility, and to properly administer and enforce the laws pertaining thereto.

The information is made available as a routine use on a need-to-know basis to personnel of the Department of State and other government agencies having statutory or other lawful authority to maintain such information in the performance of their official duties; pursuant to a subpoena or court order; and, as set forth in Part 6a, Title 22, Code of Federal Regulations (See Federal Register Volume 40, pages 45755, 45756, 47419 and 47420).

Failure to provide the information requested on this form may result in the denial of a United States Passport, related document or service to the individual seeking such passport, document or service.

NOTE: The disclosure of your Social Security Number or of the identity and location of a person to be notified in the event of death or accident is entirely voluntary. However, failure to provide this information may prevent the Department of State from providing you with timely assistance or protection in the event you should encounter an emergency situation while outside the United States.

I

ACTS OR CONDITIONS

(If any of the below-mentioned acts or conditions have been performed by or apply to the applicant, or to any other person to be included in the passport, the portion which applies should be struck out, and a supplementary explanatory statement under oath (or affirmation) by the person to whom the portion is applicable should be attached and made a part of this application.)

I have not (and no other person included in this application has), since acquiring United States citizenship, been naturalized as a citizen of a foreign state; taken an oath or made an affirmation or other formal declaration of allegiance to a foreign state; entered or served in the armed forces of a foreign state; accepted or performed the duties of any office, post, or employment under the government of a foreign state or political subdivision thereof; made a formal renunciation of nationality either in the United States or before a diplomatic or consular officer of the United States in a foreign state; or been convicted by a court or court martial of competent jurisdiction of committing any act of treason against, or attempting by force to overthrow, or bearing arms against, the United States, or conspiring to overthrow, put down or to destroy by force, the Government of the United States.

WARNING: False statements made knowingly and willfully in passport applications or in affidavits or other supporting documents submitted therewith are punishable by fine and/or imprisonment under the provisions of 18 USC 1001 and/or 18 USC 1542. Alteration or mutilation of a passport issued pursuant to this application is punishable by fine and/or imprisonment under the provisions of 18 USC 1543. The use of a passport in violation of the restrictions contained therein or of the passport regulations is punishable by fine and/or imprisonment under 18 USC 1544. All statements and documents submitted are subject to verification.

J

(FOR USE OF APPLICATION ACCEPTANCE AGENT ONLY)	
APPLICANT'S IDENTIFYING DOCUMENT(S)	IDENTIFYING DOCUMENT(S) OF WIFE/HUSBAND TO BE INCLUDED IN PASSPORT
☐ Certificate of Naturalization or Citizenship ☐ Passport ☐ Driver's License ☐ Other (Specify):	No.: Issue Date: Expiration Date: Place of Issue: Issued in Name of:
☐ Certificate of Naturalization or Citizenship ☐ Passport ☐ Driver's License ☐ Other (Specify):	No.: Issue Date: Expiration Date: Place of Issue: Issued in Name of:

139

APPLICATION FOR AMENDMENT OF PASSPORT

(SEE INSTRUCTIONS ON REVERSE)

A | **THIS SECTION MUST BE COMPLETED BY ALL APPLICANTS**

PRINT CURRENT NAME IN FULL
(First name)　　　　(Middle name)　　　　(Last name)

PASSPORT NUMBER

DATE OF ISSUE
Month　Day　Year

I, _____

a citizen of the United States, do hereby request that my passport, which is enclosed, be amended as indicated below.

MAIL PASSPORT TO:

In care of (if applicable) _____

Street _____

City _____ State _____ ZIP Code _____

Phone Nos.　Area Code _____ Home: _____ Business: _____

SEX (M-F) | BIRTHPLACE (City, State or Province, Country) | BIRTH DATE Month Day Year

DATE OF DEPARTURE | PERMANENT RESIDENCE (Street Address, City, State, ZIP Code)

STAPLE ONE PHOTO HERE. ATTACH SECOND PHOTO BY PAPER CLIP. Photos must be ONLY of persons to be included by this amendment. The two photos must be identical, 2 x 2 inches in size, be on thin, nonglossy paper with a plain, light background and have been taken within 6 months of date submitted. When 1 person is included, the image size measured from bottom of chin to top of head must be between 1 and 1-3/8 inches. Photos should be front view, but not full length. Most vending machine prints are not acceptable. When more than 1 person is to be included, a group photo is required. Color photos are acceptable. Photographs should be taken in normal street attire, without a hat. Dark glasses are not acceptable unless required for medical reasons. Photos must be signed by passport bearer on the reverse.

B | **CHANGE TO EXCLUDE:**

☐ My Wife
☐ My Husband
☐ My Child(ren) or Brother(s) and Sister(s) (Give name(s))

WHO WILL
☐ Apply for Separate Passport(s)
☐ Not Accompany Me
☐

(PASSPORT OFFICE USE ONLY)

Amend as shown in section:
☐ B　☐ C　☐ D　☐ E　☐ F
☐ Add visa pages.
☐ Endorsement _____
☐

C | **CHANGE TO INCLUDE: MY (WIFE) (HUSBAND)**

(WIFE'S) (HUSBAND'S) FULL LEGAL NAME | DATE OF BIRTH

PLACE OF BIRTH (City, State or Province, Country) | DATE OF MARRIAGE

Wife's/Husband's Birth Certificate
Filed　　　　SR　CR　City

Certificate of Naturalization or Citizenship
No.　　　　Date
Place　　　☐ Seen and Returned

Child(ren)'s Evidence of Citizenship

☐ Seen and Returned

D | **CHANGE TO INCLUDE: MY CHILD(REN) OR BROTHER(S) AND SISTER(S) UNDER THE AGE OF 13 YEARS**

NAME(S) IN FULL | PLACE(S) OF BIRTH (City, State or Country) | DATE(S) OF BIRTH

E | **CHANGE NAME:**

PASSPORT SHOULD READ AS FOLLOWS: | FORMER NAME IN PASSPORT

NAME CHANGED BY (Submit original or certified document)
☐ Marriage
☐ Court Order
☐ Other:

COMPLETE IF NAME CHANGED BY MARRIAGE:

Date of Marriage | Husband's Name in Full

Husband's Date of Birth | Husband's Place of Birth | ☐ Husband is U.S. Citizen ☐ Husband is not U.S. Citizen

COMPLETE IF NAME CHANGED BY COURT ORDER:

Name of Court | Location (City, State) | Date

I have not (and no other person included in this application has), since acquiring United States citizenship, performed any of the acts listed in section K on the reverse of this application form (unless explanatory statement is attached). I solemnly swear (or affirm) that the statements made on all of the pages of this application are true and the photograph attached is a likeness of those persons to be included in the passport.

(To be signed at same time by husband/wife to be included in passport) | (SEAL) | (To be signed by Applicant in presence of person administering oath)

Subscribed and sworn to (affirmed) before me this _____ day of _____ 19 _____.

Clerk of the _____, Postal Employee/Passport Agent at _____.

(Signature of person authorized to accept passport application)

FORM 1-78 DSP-19 | PLEASE TYPE OR PRINT CLEARLY IN INK (Pencil is not acceptable) *(OVER)* | FORM APPROVED O.M.B. NO. 47-R0069

F | **CHANGE OTHER:**

EXPLAIN

G | COMPLETE IF ANY PERSON TO BE INCLUDED HAS PREVIOUSLY BEEN ISSUED OR INCLUDED IN A U.S. PASSPORT

		NUMBER	DATE OF ISSUE
INCLUDED	☐ CHILD(REN)'S ☐ WIFE'S ☐ HUSBAND'S LAST U.S. PASSPORT		

IN NAME OF	☐ IS SUBMITTED HEREWITH
	☐ OTHER DISPOSITION (State)

H | COMPLETE IF ANY PERSON TO BE INCLUDED WAS NOT BORN IN THE U.S. AND CLAIMS CITIZENSHIP THROUGH PARENT(S)

ENTERED THE U.S. (Month) (Year)	IF FATHER NATURALIZED:		IF KNOWN, FATHER'S RESIDENCE/ PHYSICAL PRESENCE IN U.S.
☐ Wife	Date	Certificate No.	From (Year) To (Year)
☐ Husband			
☐ Child	Before (Name of Court)	Place (City, State)	

RESIDENCE/CONTINUOUS PHYSICAL PRESENCE IN U.S. From (Year) To (Year)	IF MOTHER NATURALIZED:		IF KNOWN, MOTHER'S RESIDENCE/ PHYSICAL PRESENCE IN U.S.
☐ Wife	Date	Certificate No.	From (Year) To (Year)
☐ Husband			
☐ Child	Before (Name of Court)	Place (City, State)	

I | COMPLETE IF WIFE WHO IS TO BE INCLUDED WAS PREVIOUSLY MARRIED BEFORE MARCH 3, 1931 (Women applicants must also complete if children of a previous marriage are to be included)

WIFE'S MAIDEN NAME	DATE OF PREVIOUS MARRIAGE	FULL NAME OF FORMER HUSBAND

FORMER HUSBAND'S PLACE OF BIRTH	FORMER HUSBAND'S DATE OF BIRTH	☐ FORMER HUSBAND WAS U.S. CITIZEN	PREVIOUS MARRIAGE TERMINATED BY
		☐ FORMER HUSBAND WAS NOT U.S. CITIZEN	☐ Death ☐ Divorce on (Date)

J | IN THE EVENT OF DEATH OR ACCIDENT NOTIFY (Do not show name of a person who will accompany you when traveling) (Not Mandatory)

NAME IN FULL	RELATIONSHIP

STREET ADDRESS, CITY, STATE, ZIP CODE	PHONE NO.

K | **ACTS OR CONDITIONS**

(If any of the below-mentioned acts or conditions have been performed by or apply to the applicant, or to any other person included or to be included in the passport, the portion which applies should be struck out and a supplementary explanatory statement under oath (or affirmation) by the person to whom the portion is applicable should be attached and made a part of this application.)

I have not (and no other person included or to be included in the passport has), since acquiring United States citizenship, been naturalized as a citizen of a foreign state; taken an oath or made an affirmation or other formal declaration of allegiance to a foreign state; entered or served in the armed forces of a foreign state; accepted or performed the duties of any office, post, or employment under the government of a foreign state or political subdivision thereof; made a formal renunciation of nationality either in the United States or before a diplomatic or consular officer of the United States in a foreign state; ever sought or claimed the benefits of the nationality of any foreign state; or been convicted by a court or court martial of competent jurisdiction of committing any act of treason against, or attempting by force to overthrow, or bearing arms against, the United States, or conspiring to overthrow, put down or to destroy by force, the Government of the United States.

WARNING: False statements made knowingly and willfully in passport applications or affidavits or other supporting documents are punishable by fine and/or imprisonment under the provisions of 18 USC 1001 and/or 18 USC 1542.

L | (FOR USE OF APPLICATION ACCEPTANCE AGENT ONLY)

IDENTIFYING DOCUMENT SUBMITTED (Proper evidence to identify the husband/wife to be included in the passport must be submitted)

☐ Certificate of Naturalization or Citizenship	No.:	Place of Issue:
☐ Passport	Issue Date:	Issued in Name of:
☐ Driver's License	Expiration Date:	
☐ Other (Specify):		

INSTRUCTIONS: A passport may be amended at the request of the bearer to show a change of name, to correct the descriptive data, to include a wife/husband, to include children or brothers and sisters under the age of 13 years, or to exclude a person previously included. A passport may not be amended to exclude the bearer or to reinclude a person previously excluded from the passport.

This application must be executed before a Clerk of Court accepting applications, or a Postal Employee designated by the postmaster at a post office which has been selected to accept passport applications, or a Passport Agent when a person is to be included. A wife/husband to be included must appear with the bearer to execute and sign the application. Children under the age of 13 years to be included are not required to appear. (NOTE: A person included in the passport of another may not use the passport for travel unless he is accompanied by the bearer.) Evidence of citizenship and photographs which meet the requirements shown in the photograph block must be submitted for all persons to be included. Documentary evidence such as a certified court order, a marriage certificate or other satisfactory evidence of marriage, must be submitted to support a change of name.

PRIVACY ACT STATEMENT: The information solicited on this form is authorized by, but not limited to, those statutes codified in Titles 8, 18, and 22, United States Code, and all predecessor statutes whether or not codified, and all regulations issued pursuant to Executive Order 11295 of August 5, 1966. The primary purpose for soliciting the information is to establish citizenship, identity and entitlement to issuance of a United States passport or related facility, and to properly administer and enforce the laws pertaining thereto.

The information is made available as a routine use on a need-to-know basis to personnel of the Department of State and other Government agencies having statutory or other lawful authority to maintain such information in the performance of their official duties; pursuant to a subpoena or court order; and, as set forth in Part 6a, Title 22, Code of Federal Regulations (See Federal Register Volume 40, pages 45755, 45756, 47419 and 47420).

Failure to provide the information requested on this form may result in the denial of a United States passport, related document or service to the individual seeking such passport, document or service.

U.S. GOVERNMENT PRINTING OFFICE   +48—16—84318-1

DEPARTMENT OF STATE
APPLICATION FOR PASSPORT BY MAIL
Your most recent passport issued within the past eight years,
two signed photographs and the fee of $10 MUST accompany this application.

(PASSPORT OFFICE USE ONLY)
Endorsement _____

(First name)   (Middle name)   (Last name)

I, _____
a citizen of the United States, do hereby apply to the Department of State for a passport.

MAIL PASSPORT TO:

IN CARE OF (If applicable) _____

STREET _____

CITY _____ STATE _____ ZIP CODE _____

PHONE NOS. Area Code: _____ Home: _____ Business: _____

SEX ☐ Male ☐ Female	BIRTHPLACE (City, State or Province, Country)		BIRTH DATE Month | Day | Year
HEIGHT ___ FT. ___ IN.	COLOR OF HAIR (Spell out)	COLOR OF EYES (Spell out)	OCCUPATION
DATE OF DEPARTURE		VISIBLE DISTINGUISHING MARKS	

EVIDENCE OF NAME CHANGE

Type _____
Date _____
Place _____
From _____
To _____

MOST RECENT PASSPORT ISSUED WITHIN PAST 8 YEARS MUST BE ATTACHED
No. _____ Issue Date _____

SOCIAL SECURITY NUMBER (Not Mandatory)

PERMANENT RESIDENCE (Street Address, City, State, ZIP Code)	COUNTY OF RESIDENCE (Not Mandatory)	IF YOU WERE BORN ABROAD, WERE YOUR PARENTS U.S. CITIZENS AT THE TIME OF YOUR BIRTH? Father: ☐ Yes ☐ No Mother: ☐ Yes ☐ No

IN THE EVENT OF ACCIDENT OR DEATH NOTIFY (Not Mandatory) (Do not show name of person who will travel with you)

Name in full: Relationship:
Address: Phone No.:

PROPOSED TRAVEL PLANS (For Statistical Reporting Purposes — Not Mandatory)

PURPOSE OF TRIP	MEANS OF TRANSPORTATION			COUNTRIES TO BE VISITED
		Sea	Air	Other
PROPOSED LENGTH OF STAY	Departure	☐	☐	☐
	Return	☐	☐	☐
	DO YOU EXPECT TO TAKE ANOTHER TRIP ABROAD?			
NO. OF PREVIOUS TRIPS ABROAD WITHIN LAST 12 MONTHS	☐ Yes ☐ No IF SO, WITHIN ☐ 1 year ☐ 2 years ☐ 5 years			

(If any of the below-mentioned acts or conditions have been performed by or apply to the applicant, the portion which applies should be struck out, and a supplementary explanatory statement should be attached, signed and made a part of this application.)

I have not since acquiring United States citizenship, been naturalized as a citizen of a foreign state; taken an oath, or made an affirmation or other formal declaration of allegiance to a foreign state; entered or served in the armed forces of a foreign state; accepted or performed the duties of any office, post, or employment under the Government of a foreign state or political subdivision thereof; made a formal renunciation of nationality either in the United States or before a diplomatic or consular officer of the United States in a foreign state; or been convicted by a court or court martial of competent jurisdiction of committing any act of treason against, or attempting by force to overthrow, put down or to destroy by force the Government of the United States.

WARNING: False statements made knowingly and willfully in passport applications or affidavits or other supporting documents are punishable by fine and/or imprisonment, under the provisions of 18 USC 1001 and/or 18 USC 1542. The alteration or mutilation of a passport issued pursuant to this application is punishable by fine and/or imprisonment under 18 USC 1543. The use of a passport in violation of the restrictions therein is punishable by fine and/or imprisonment under 18 USC 1544.

DECLARATION: I declare that the statements made in this application are true and complete to the best of my knowledge and belief, that the attached photographs are a true likeness of me, and that I have not been issued or included in a passport issued subsequent to the one submitted herein.

_____   _____
(Date)   (Signature of applicant)

(PASSPORT OFFICE USE ONLY)

2" X 2"
FROM 1" TO 1-3/8"

Submit two identical signed photographs which meet all requirements in paragraph 2 on reverse.

FORM DSP-82
7-79

Please type or print clearly in ink (pencil is not acceptable). Please recheck the application and enclosures before mailing. Incomplete or improperly prepared applications will cause delay in the issuance of your passport.

Form Approved:
OMB NO. 47–R0172

Form DSP-82
7-79

APPLICATION FOR PASSPORT BY MAIL

IMPORTANT: You may use this application ONLY IF:

- You have been the bearer of a passport issued within eight years prior to the date of your new application; and
- You are able to submit your most recent U.S. passport with your new application; and
- Your previous passport was *not* issued before your 18th birthday; and
- You are *not* applying for an Official, Diplomatic or no-fee passport; and
- You do *not* wish to include a member of your family in your new passport.

If you do not meet all of the above provisions, you MUST complete a regular Passport Application, Form DSP-11. Form DSP-11 must be PERSONALLY presented to and executed by: A Passport Agent; a clerk of any Federal court or State court of record, or a judge or clerk of any probate court, accepting applications; or a postal employee designated by the postmaster at a post office which has been selected to accept passport applications.

NOTE: This application may not be used by persons outside the United States. Passports may not be mailed to private addresses outside the United States.

INFORMATION FOR PERSONS ELIGIBLE TO APPLY FOR A PASSPORT BY MAIL

1. **PROCEDURE FOR APPLYING FOR A PASSPORT BY MAIL.** If you have your MOST RECENT passport which was issued in your own name within the past 8 years, and you wish to obtain a new passport, complete and forward this application to the nearest Passport Agency listed below. You need NOT appear in person. THE APPLICATION MUST BE ACCOMPANIED BY YOUR MOST RECENT PASSPORT, TWO RECENT SIGNED PHOTOGRAPHS, AND THE PASSPORT FEE OF $10. A passport will be issued only in the name in which your previous passport was issued unless the application is also accompanied by an original or certified court order or marriage certificate reflecting the change in name. These documents will be returned with your new passport. *If you are planning to travel abroad extensively, be sure to order a 48-page passport.* Remember, if your case does not come within all of the circumstances noted under IMPORTANT, you must apply on Form DSP-11.

2. **PHOTOGRAPHS.** TWO RECENT IDENTICAL SIGNED PHOTOGRAPHS must be submitted with this application. They must be 2 x 2 inches in size. The image size measured from the bottom of the chin to the top of the head (including hair) must be not less than 1 inch nor more than 1-3/8 inches. The photographs must be signed in the center on the reverse. The signature on the photographs must agree with the signature on the application. Photographs may be in color or in black and white. A pleasant, natural pose is recommended. The prints should be capable of withstanding a mounting temperature of up to 225 degrees Fahrenheit (107 degrees Celsius) for 30 seconds. MOST VENDING MACHINE PRINTS ARE NOT ACCEPTABLE. TINTED PHOTOGRAPHS ARE NOT ACCEPTABLE. Photographs must be on thin, preferably nonglossy paper, and show a front view of you with a plain, light background. Photographs should be taken in normal street attire, without a hat. Dark glasses are not acceptable unless required for medical reasons. Only applicants who are in the active service of the Armed Forces and who are proceeding abroad in the discharge of their duties may submit photographs in the uniform of the Armed Forces of the United States.

3. **PASSPORT FEE.** THE FEE OF $10 IN CHECK OR MONEY ORDER MADE PAYABLE TO THE PASSPORT OFFICE MUST BE ENCLOSED WITH YOUR APPLICATION. If you desire special postal service other than first class mail (registered, special delivery), include the appropriate fees. DO NOT SEND CASH. The Passport Office cannot accept responsibility for cash sent through the mail. A separate check or money order should be submitted with each application.

4. **REQUESTS FOR OTHER PASSPORT SERVICES.** Requests for passport services such as change in name, inclusion of children under the age of 13 years, extension of validity and questions regarding nationality should be addressed to the nearest Passport Agency.

5. **ADDRESSES OF PASSPORT AGENCIES**

Boston Passport Agency
Room E123, John F. Kennedy Bldg.
Government Center
Boston, MA 02203

Chicago Passport Agency
Suite 380, Kluczynski Federal Bldg.
230 South Dearborn Street
Chicago, IL 60604

Detroit Passport Agency
Suite 1900, McNamara Federal Bldg.
477 Michigan Avenue
Detroit, MI 48226

Honolulu Passport Agency
Room C-106, New Federal Bldg.
300 Ala Moana Boulevard
P.O. Box 50185
Honolulu, HI 96850

Houston Passport Agency
One Allen Center
500 Dallas Street
Houston, TX 77002

Los Angeles Passport Agency
Room 2W16, Hawthorne Federal Bldg.
15000 Aviation Boulevard
Lawndale, CA 90261

Miami Passport Agency
Room 804, Federal Office Bldg.
51 S.W. First Avenue
Miami, FL 33130

New Orleans Passport Agency
Room 400, International Trade Mart
2 Canal Street
New Orleans, LA 70130

New York Passport Agency
Room 270, Rockefeller Center
630 Fifth Avenue
New York, NY 10020

Philadelphia Passport Agency
Room 4426, Federal Bldg.
600 Arch Street
Philadelphia, PA 19106

San Francisco Passport Agency
Room 1405, Federal Bldg.
450 Golden Gate Avenue
San Francisco, CA 94102

Seattle Passport Agency
Room 906, Federal Bldg.
915 Second Avenue
Seattle, WA 98174

Stamford Passport Agency
One Landmark Square
Broad and Atlantic Streets
Stamford, CT 06901

Washington Passport Agency
1425 K Street, N.W.
Washington, DC 20524

PRIVACY ACT STATEMENT

The information solicited on this form is authorized by, but not limited to, those statutes codified in Titles 8, 18, and 22, United States Code, and all predecessor statutes whether or not codified, and all regulations issued pursuant to Executive Order 11295 of August 5, 1966. The primary purpose for soliciting the information is to establish citizenship, identity and entitlement to issuance of a United States passport or related facility, and to properly administer and enforce the laws pertaining thereto.

The information is made available as a routine use on a need-to-know basis to personnel of the Department of State and other government agencies having statutory or other lawful authority to maintain such information in the performance of their official duties; pursuant to a subpoena or court order; and, as set forth in Part 6a, Title 22, Code of Federal Regulations (See Federal Register Volume 40, pages 45755, 45756, 47419 and 47420).

Failure to provide the information requested on this form may result in the denial of a United States passport, related document or service to the individual seeking such passport, document or service.

NOTE: The disclosure of your Social Security Number or of the identity and location of a person to be notified in the event of death or accident is entirely voluntary. However, failure to provide this information may prevent the Department of State from providing you with timely assistance or protection in the event you should encounter an emergency situation while outside the United States.

(GPO : 1979 O - 296-262

Chapter 12

Information Sources for Administrator and Expatriate

The greater our knowledge increases, the greater our ignorance unfolds.

—John F. Kennedy

THE FOLLOWING RECOMMENDATIONS are based purely on my own knowledge of what is available in the market place. None of the following companies have asked for, paid for, or in any way solicited inclusion in this book.

General Consulting Services

Many new consulting companies have entered the arena of international compensation and policies in recent years. However, the following institutions have been providing services to multinational companies in excess of fifteen years. For information on general international policies, commodities and services allowances, housing allowances, tax tables, surveys, seminars, counseling, etc., I suggest you contact one of the following (in alphabetical order):

Associates for International Research Inc. (AIRINC)
1100 Massachusetts Ave.
Cambridge, Mass. 02138
Tel: (617) 354-2133

The Conference Board, Inc.
845 Third Avenue
New York, N.Y. 10022
Tel: (212) 759-0900

Organization Resources Counselors
Rockefeller Center, 1211 Avenue of the Americas
New York, N.Y. 10036
Tel: (212) 575-7500

On a smaller scale:
International Compensation Inc. (INCOM)
Suite 340, Two Center Plaza
Boston, Mass. 02108
Tel: (617) 227-9760

Business International Corporation
One Dag Hammarskjold Plaza
New York, N.Y. 10017
Tel: (212) 750-6300

National Foreign Trade Council
10 Rockefeller Plaza
New York, N.Y. 10020
Tel: (212) 581-6200

Job Evaluations

A good job evaluation process yields a common language for discussing compensation, job content, and related issues. It also facilitates interchanges of personnel among subsidiaries, both domestic and international. To secure more information on job evaluation and correlation, both domestic and international, contact:

Hay Associates
229 South 18th St.
Philadelphia, Penn. 19103
Tel: (215) 875-2300

Taxation Advice

Most reputable international public accounting firms have departments, both in the United States and overseas, which are geared to providing expatriate tax advice and the preparation of tax returns. I suggest you first approach the CPA firm which handles your corporate accounts. If they are not satisfactory, you might try Arthur Young & Company. I have used them for fifteen years and have found their service to be both competent and efficient. They have offices in all countries to which I have been assigned; if they do not have a resident office, they will send a CPA from the nearest branch.

Arthur Young and Company,
277 Park Avenue,
New York, N.Y. 10017
Phone (212) 922-2000

Try to get hold of their 117-page booklet entitled "Taxation of U.S. Expatriates." It is superbly designed to familiarize expatriates with the unique and complicated federal tax provisions and rules that apply to them while overseas. The book contains examples of the application of certain rules and also includes answers to the tax questions most frequently asked by expatriates.

Detailed Information on Host Countries

Information on individual countries—the country, economy, climate, language, religion, laws, visa requirements, work and residence permits, health requirements, vaccinations, customs regulations, entry requirements for pets, transportation, hotels, currency, banks, taxes, time differences, business hours, holidays, housing, schools, leisure activities, etc.—can be acquired by writing to:

Director
Overseas Assignment Directory Service
Knowledge Industry Publications Inc.
2 Corporate Park Drive
White Plains, N.Y. 10604
Tel: (914) 694-8686

This directory is the who, what, and where handbook for expatriates and international travelers. I recommend it for all personnel administrators who are involved with orientation and training of expatriates.

Published Material on International Compensation

Business International, in addition to supplying COL indexes, research and publish material in the area of executive compensation and consultation, as well as useful overseas labor relations material (*Business Asia, Business Europe,* etc.). For a complete list of their services, write to:

Business International Corporation
One Dag Hammarskjold Plaza
New York, N.Y. 10017
Tel: (212) 750-6300

Publications on Business Management

AMACOM is the in-house publishing division of the American Management Association. They have a worldwide reputation as the largest publisher of business books, periodicals, newsletters, cassette programs, and survey reports. For information on publications and surveys that would give further insight into your expatriate policy and compensation area and most other areas of management education, write to:

The American Management Association
135 West 50th Street
New York, N.Y. 10020
Tel: (212) 586-8100

Personalized Orientations

The following company offers highly personalized, unbiased and intelligent family counseling, and predeparture and post-arrival orientations—these include a review of the culture, politics, and economy of the country; the management environment; and the availability of housing, schooling, medical facilities, and community services. These services are ideal for companies that do not have in-house relocation expertise or would prefer an independent viewpoint which relieves them from involvement in personal affairs.

> IRC Counsellors Ltd.
> 2 Queen Anne Mews
> Chandos Street
> London WIM 9 DF.
> Tel: (UK): 01-636-9436
> Telex: 299078

Legal Representation Abroad

To find a lawyer abroad, a list of attorneys by country may be obtained from the U.S. Commerce Department at the following address:

> Office of Export Development
> Bureau of International Commerce
> U.S. Commerce Department
> Washington, D.C. 20230
> Tel: (202) 377-2000

or, from:

> International Bar Association (U.S. branch)
> 2100 The Fidelity Bldg.
> Philadelphia, Penn. 19109
> Tel: (215) 491-9200

Accredited Physicians Overseas

Establishing contact with a qualified, English-speaking physician abroad can be expedited by contacting one of the following organizations prior to departure:

Intermedic
777 Third Avenue
New York, N.Y. 10017
Tel: (212) 486-8974

IAMAT
350 Fifth Avenue
New York, N.Y. 10118
Tel: (212) 279-6465

Driving Information

For particulars about driving conditions and necessary permits and licences for operating a vehicle overseas, contact:

American Automobile Association
8111 Gatehouse Road
Falls Church, Va. 22047
Tel: (703) 222-6000

Information Regarding Pets

For country-by-country regulations regarding entry requirements for pets, contact:

American Society for the Prevention of
    Cruelty to Animals (ASPCA)
441 East 92nd Street
New York, N.Y. 10028
Tel: (212) 876-7700

Some Useful Data Sources—Pre- and Post-Relocation

Many associations and institutes around the world publish brochures and handbooks that help prepare prospective expatriates for adjustment to a new environment. The American

Women's Club, for example, can be contacted in care of most U.S. embassies around the world or at Drive du Caporal 13A, 1180 Brussels, Belgium. Probably the best sources of information, however, are the embassy staff themselves, both United States and foreign; the following addresses and telephone numbers might prove useful in this regard:

Algeria

U.S. Embassy
4 Chemin Cheich Bachir Brahimi
B.P. Box 549 (Alger-Gare),
   Algiers
Tel. 601425/601255/601186
601716/601828
Telex 52064

Embassy of Algeria
2118 Kalorama Road N.W.
Washington, D.C. 20008
Tel. (202) 234-7246

Argentina

U.S. Embassy
4300 Colombia, 1425
Buenos Aires, Argentina
Tel. 774-7611/8811/9911
(or APO Miami 34034)

Dirección Nacional da Turismo
Calle Suipacha 1111
Buenos Aires, Argentina

Embassy of Argentina
1600 N. Hampshire Ave. N.W.
Washington, D.C. 20009
Tel. (202) 387-0705

Australia

U.S. Embassy
Moonah Place
Canberra, A.C.T. 2600
Australia
Tel. (062) 73-7311
Telex AA62104
(or APO San Francisco 96404)

Embassy of Australia
1601 Massachusetts Ave. N.W.
Washington, D.C. 20036
Tel. (202) 797-3000

Austria

U.S. Embassy
Boltzmanngasse 16A
1019 Vienna, Austria
Tel. (222) 31-55-11
Telex 74634

Embassy of Austria
2343 Massachusetts Ave. N.W.
Washington, D.C. 20008
Tel. (202) 483-4474

Austrian Consulate General
  (and information service)
31 E. 69th St.
New York, N.Y. 10021
Tel. (212) 737-6400

Bahrain
  U.S. Embassy
  Shalkh Isa Road
  P.O. Box 26431
  Manama, Bahrain
  Tel. 714151/713323
  (or FPO NY 09526)

Embassy of the State of Bahrain
2600 Virginia Ave. N.W.
Suite 715
Washington, D.C. 20037
Tel. (202) 965-4930

Bahrain Mission to U.N.
747 Third Ave.
New York, N.Y. 10017
Tel. (212) 751-8805

Bangladesh
  U.S. Embassy
  Adamjee Court Bldg.
  (5th Floor), GPO Box 323
  Motijheel, Dacca
  Bangladesh
  Tel: 244220 through 244229

Embassy of Bangladesh
3421 Massachusetts Ave. N.W.
Washington, D.C. 20007
Tel: (202) 337-6644

Belgium
  U.S. Embassy
  27 Blvd du Regent
  B-1000 Brussels, Belgium
  Tel: 513 3830
  Telex 846 21336
  or APO NY 09667

Belgium Embassy
3330 Garfield St. N.W.
Washington, D.C. 20008
Tel: (202) 333-6900

  American Womens Club
  16 Rue du College Saint Michael
  1150 Brussels, Belgium

Belgium National Tourist Office
720 Fifth Ave.
New York, N.Y. 10019
Tel: (212) 582-1750

Bolivia
  U.S. Embassy
  Banco Popular Del Peru Bldg.
    Corner of Calles Mercado and
    Colon
  P.O. Box 425
  La Paz, Bolivia
  Tel: 350251
  Telex BX5240
  (or APO Miami 34032)

Embassy of Bolivia
1625 Massachusetts Ave. N.W.
  Suite 600
Washington, D.C. 20036
Tel: (202) 483-4410

Brazil
U.S. Embassy
Lote 3 Avenida das Nocoes
Brazilia, Brazil
Tel: 2230120
Telex 061 1091
(or APO Miami 34030)

Brazilian Embassy
3006 Massachusetts Ave. N.W.
Washington, D. C. 20008
Tel: (202) 797-0100

U.S. Consulate-General
Avenida Presidente Wilson 147
Rio de Janeiro, Brazil
Tel: 2528055/56/57

Brazilian Consulate-General
630 Fifth Ave.
New York, N.Y. 10020
Tel: (212) 757-3080

Burma
U.S. Embassy
581 Merchant St.
Rangoon, Burma
Tel: 18055

Embassy of the Union of Burma
2300 S. St. N.W.
Washington, D.C. 20008
Tel: (202) 332-9044

Canada
U.S. Embassy
100 Wellington St. KIP 5TI
Ottawa, Canada
Tel: (613) 238-5335
Telex 0533582

Canadian Embassy
1746 Massachusetts Ave. N.W.
Washington, D.C. 20036
Tel: (202) 785-1400

Chile
U.S. Embassy
Codina Bldg.
Augustinas 1343
7° Santiago, Chile
Tel: 710133/90 & 710326/75
Telex 40062-ICA-CL
(or APO Miami 34033)

Embassy of Chile
1732 Massachusetts Ave. N.W.
Washington, D.C. 20036
Tel: (202) 785-1746

Colombia
U.S. Embassy
Calle 37, No. 8-40
Bogotá, Colombia
Tel: 285-1300
Telex 44843
(or APO Miami 34038)

Embassy of Colombia
2118 Leroy Place N.W.
Washington, D.C. 20008
Tel: (202) 387-5828

Cyprus
U.S. Embassy
Therissos St. and Dositheos St.
Nicosia, Cyprus
Tel: 65151/5
(or FPO NY 09530)

Embassy of Cyprus
2211 R. St. N.W.
Washington, D.C. 20008
Tel: (202) 462-5772
    (202) 232-7217

Denmark
  U.S. Embassy
  Dag Hammarskjolds Allé 24
  2100 Copenhagen, Denmark
  Tel: (01) 42.31.44
  Telex 22216
  (or APO NY 09170

Embassy of Denmark
3200 Whitehaven, N.W.
Washington, D.C. 20008
Tel: (202) 234-4300

Danish Information Office
588 Fifth Avenue
New York, N.Y. 10036
Tel: (212) 582-2802

Ecuador
  U.S. Embassy
  120 Avenida Patria
  Quito, Ecuador
  Tel: 548-000
  (or APO Miami 34039)

Embassy of Ecuador
2535 15th St. N.W.
Washington, D.C. 20009
Tel: (202) 234-7200

Egypt
  U.S. Embassy
  5 Sharia Latin America
  P.O. Box 10
  Cairo, Egypt
  Tel: 28211 through 28219
  (or FPO NY 09527)
  Telex 93773
  (American Women's Club
    care of above)

Embassy of the
  Arab Republic of Egypt
2310 Decatur Place, N.W.
Washington, D.C. 20008
Tel: (202) 234-3903/232-5400

  U.S. Consulate
  110 Ave. Horreya
  Alexandria, Egypt
  Tel: 801911/25607
  (or FPO NY 09527)

Egyptian Consulate-General
36 E. 67th St.
New York, N.Y. 10021
Tel: (212) 759-7120

El Salvador
  U.S. Embassy
  25 Avda. Norte 1230
  San Salvador, El Salvador
  Tel: 26-7100
  (or APO Miami 34023)

Embassy of El Salvador
2308 California St. N.W.
Washington, D.C. 20008
Tel: (202) 265-3480

Finland

U.S. Embassy
Itäinen Puistotie 14A
Helsinki, Finland
Tel: 171931
Telex 121644 USEMB SF
(or APO NY 09664)

Embassy of Finland
1900 24th St. N.W.
Washington, D.C. 20008
Tel: (202) 462-0556

France

U.S. Embassy
2 Ave Gabriel
Paris 8, France
Tel: 2961202, 2618075
Telex 650-221
(or APO NY 09777)

Embassy of France
2535 Belmont Road N.W.
Washington, D.C. 20008
Tel: (202) 234-0990

American Womens Club
49 rue Pierre Charoon
Paris 8, France

French Consulate-General
934 Fifth Ave.
New York, N.Y. 10021
Tel: (212) 535-0100

Germany

U.S. Embassy
Delchmannsaue
5300 Bonn 2
W. Germany
Tel: 02221-8955
Telex 885452
(or APO NY 09080)

Embassy of the
    Federal Republic of Germany
4645 Reservoir Road N.W.
Washington, D.C. 20007
Tel: (202) 331-3000

U.S. Consulate
Seismayerstrasse 21
6000 Frankfurt
Tel: (0611) 74 50 04
(or APO NY 09757)

German Consulate-General
460 Park Ave.
New York, N.Y. 10022
Tel: (212) 688-3523

American Chamber of
    Commerce
Rossmarket, 12
6000 Frankfurt/Main
W. Germany

German Information Center
410 Park Ave.
New York, N.Y. 10022
Tel: (212) 688-3523

Greece

U.S. Embassy
91 Vasilissi Sophia Blvd.
Athens, Greece
Tel: 712951, 718401
Telex 21-5548
(or APO NY 09253)

U.S. Consulate-General
59 Vasileos Constantinou
Thessaloniki, Greece
Tel: 266-121
(or APO NY 09693)

Embassy of Greece
2221 Massachusetts Ave. N.W.
Washington, D.C. 20008
Tel: (202) 667-3168

Greek National Tourist
    Organization
150 E. 58th St.
New York, N.Y. 10022
Tel: (212) 421-5777

Guatemala

U.S. Embassy
Avda de la Reforma 7-01
Zona 10
Guatemala City, Guatemala
Tel: 31-15-41
(or APO Miami 34024)

Embassy of Guatemala
2220 R. St. N.W.
Washington, D.C. 20008
Tel: (202) 332-2865

Consulate of Guatemala
1270 Avenue of the Americas
New York, N.Y. 10020
Tel: (212) 246-5877

India

U.S. Embassy
Shanti Path
Chanakyapuri 21
New Delhi 110021, India
Tel: 690351
Telex USCS IN 031-4589

Indian Embassy and
    Information Service
2107 Massachusetts Ave. N.W.
Washington, D.C. 20008
Tel: (202) 265-5050

Indonesia

U.S. Embassy
Medan Merdeka Selatan 5
Jakarta, Indonesia
Tel: 340001/9
Telex 44218 AMEMB JKT
(or APO SF 96356)
American Women's Assoc.
Agape House
Jalan Wijaya 11/72
Kebayoran, Jakarta
Indonesia

Embassy of the
    Republic of Indonesia
2020 Massachusetts Ave. N.W.
Washington, D.C. 20036
Tel: (202) 293-1745

Consulate-General of Indonesia
    and Indonesian Information
    Service
5 E. 68th St.
New York, N.Y. 10021
Tel: (212) 879-0600

Israel
U.S. Embassy
71 Hayarkon St
Tel-Aviv, Israel
Tel: 654338
Telex 33376
(or APO NY 09672)

Embassy of Israel
1621 22nd St. N.W.
Washington, D.C. 20008
Tel: (202) 483-4100

Italy
U.S. Embassy
Via Veneto 119-A
Rome, Italy 00187
Tel: (06) 4674
Telex 610450 AMEMBRO
USICA
(or APO NY 09794)

Embassy of Italy
1601 Fuller St. N.W.
Washington, D.C. 20008
Tel: (202) 234-1935

Japan
U.S. Embassy
10-5, Akasaka 1-chome
Minato-ku, Tokyo, Japan
Tel: 5837141
Telex 2422118
(or APO San Francisco 96503)

Embassy of Japan
2520 Massachusetts Ave. N.W.
Washington, D.C. 20008
Tel: (202) 234-2266

American Chamber of
  Commerce
701 Tosho Building
2020 Marunouchi
30-chome, Chiyodaka
Tokyo 100, Japan
Tel: 2115861

Japan National Tourist
  Association
45 Rockefeller Plaza
New York, N.Y. 10020
Tel: (212) 757-5640

Korea
U.S. Embassy
82 Sejong-Ro
Chongno-gu
Seoul, S. Korea
Tel: 72-2601 through 72-2619
(or APO SF 96301)

Embassy of the
  Republic of Korea
2320 Masachusetts Ave. N.W.
Washington, D.C. 20008
Tel: (202) 483-7383

American Chamber of
  Commerce
Suite 529, Bando Bldg.
Seoul, S. Korea

Consulate-General of the
  Republic of Korea and
  National Tourist Bureau
460 Park Ave.
New York, N.Y. 10022
Tel: (212) 752-1700/688-7543

Kuwait
U.S. Embassy
P.O. Box 77, SAFAT
Kuwait City, Kuwait
Tel: 424-1519

Embassy of the State of Kuwait
2940 Tilden St. N.W.
Washington, D.C. 20008
Tel: (202) 966-0702

Ministry of Information
P.O. Box 13
Kuwait City, Kuwait

Consulate-General of Kuwait
801 2nd Ave.
New York, N.Y. 10017
Tel: (212) 661-1580

Lebanon
U.S. Embassy
Corniche at Rue
   Ain Mreisseh
Beirut, Lebanon
Tel: 361-800; 366-538; 365-463

Embassy of Lebanon
2560 28th St. N.W.
Washington, D.C. 20008
Tel: (202) 462-8600

Lebanon Tourist Office
527 Madison Ave.
New York, N.Y. 10022
Tel: (212) 421-2201

Libya
U.S. Embassy
Shari Mohammad Thabit
P.O. Box 289
Tripoli, Libya
Tel: 34021/6

Libyan Embassy
1118 22nd St. N.W.
Washington, D.C. 20037
Tel: (202) 452-1290

Malaysia
U.S. Embassy
AIA Building
Jalan Ampang, P.O. Box 35
Kuala Lumpur, Malaysia
Tel: 26321

Embassy of the
   Federation of Malaysia
2401 Massachusetts Ave. N.W.
Washington, D.C. 20008
Tel: (202) 234-7600

Malta
U.S. Embassy
Development House
2nd Floor
St. Anne Street
Floriana, Malta
Tel: 623653, 620424

Embassy of Malta
2017 Connecticut Ave. N.W.
Washington, D.C. 20008
Tel: (202) 462-3611

Mexico

U.S. Embassy
Paseo de la Reforma 305
Colonia Cuauhtemoc
Mexico City, Mexico 5 DF
Tel: 553 3333
Telex 017-73-091 & 017-75-685

Embassy of Mexico
2829 16th St. N.W.
Washington, D.C. 20009
Tel: (202) 234-6000/234-0442

Ministry of Tourism
Avda Juaréz 92
Mexico City, Mexico

Consulate-General of Mexico
8 E, 41st St.
New York, N.Y. 10017
Tel: (212) 689-0456

Morrocco

U.S. Embassy
2 ave de Marrakech, Box 120
Rabat, Morrocco
Tel: 30361/62
Telex 31005

Embassy of Morocco
1601 21st St. N.W.
Washington, D.C. 20009
Tel: (202) 462-7979

Netherland

U.S. Embassy
Lange Voorhout 102
The Hague, Netherlands
Tel: 62-49-11
Telex (044) 31016
(or APO NY 09159)

Embassy of the Netherlands
4200 Linnean Ave. N.W.
Washington, D.C. 20008
Tel: (202) 244-5300

New Zealand

U.S. Embassy
29 Fitzherbert Terrace
Thorndon, P.O. Box 1190
Wellington, New Zealand
Tel: 722-068
Telex NZ 3305
(or FPO San Francisco 96690)

New Zealand Embassy
19 Observatory Circle N.W.
Washington, D.C. 20008
Tel: (202) 265-1721

Nigeria

U.S. Embassy
2 Eleke Crescent
P.O. Box 554
Lagos, Nigeria
Tel: 610097
Nigerian Tourist Assoc.
P.O. Box 2944
47 Marina
Lagos, Nigeria

Nigerian Embassy
2201 M. St. N.W.
Washington, D.C. 20037
Tel: (202) 223-9300

Consulate-General of Nigeria
575 Lexington Ave.
New York, N.Y. 10022
Tel: (212) 752-1670

Norway
  U.S. Embassy
  Drammensveien 18
  Oslo 1, Norway
  Tel: 566880
  Telex 18470
  (or APO NY 09085)

  Norwegian Embassy
  2720 34th St. N.W.
  Washington, D.C. 20008
  Tel: (202) 333-6000

  Norwegian-American
    Chamber of Commerce
  Drammensveien 40
  Oslo 2, Norway

  Norwegian Information Service
  825 Third Ave.
  New York, N.Y. 10022
  Tel: (212) 421-7333

Pakistan
  U.S. Embassy
  Temporarily located in
    AID/UN Bldg.
  Tel: 24071

  Embassy of Pakistan
  2315 Massachusetts Ave. N.W.
  Washington, D.C. 20008
  Tel: (202) 332-8330

Panama
  U.S. Embassy
  Avda. Balboa y Calle 38
  Apdo 6959, R.P.5
  Panamá
  Tel: 27-1777

  Embassy of Panama
  2862 McGill Terrace N.W.
  Washington, D.C. 20008
  Tel: (202) 483-1407

Qatar
  U.S. Embassy
  Fariq Bin Omran (opp. TV
    station)
  P.O. Box 2399
  Doha, Qatar
  Tel: 870701/2/3

  Embassy of Qatar
  Suite 1180
  600 New Hampshire Ave. N.W.
  Washington, D.C. 20037
  Tel: (202) 338-0111

  Ministry of Information
  P.O. Box 1836
  Doha, Qatar

  Consulate-General of Qatar
  747 Third Ave.
  New York, N.Y. 10017
  Tel: (212) 486-9335

Saudi Arabia
  U.S. Embassy
  Palestine Rd., Ruwais
  Jeddah, Saudi Arabia
  Tel: 670080
  Telex 401459 AMEMB SJ
  (or APO NY 09697)

  Embassy of Saudi Arabia
  1520 18th St. N.W.
  Washington, D.C. 20036
  Tel: (202) 483-2100

Commercial Office
P.O. Box 149
Jeddah, Saudi Arabia
Tel: 670040

Singapore
U.S. Embassy
30 Hill St.
Singapore 0617
Tel: 30251
(or APO SF 96699)

South Africa
U.S. Embassy
7th Floor, Thibault House
Pretorius St. 225
Pretoria, South Africa
Tel: 48-4266
Telex 3-751

Spain
U.S. Embassy
Serrano 75
Madrid, Spain
Tel: 276-3400/3600
Telex 27763
(or APO NY 09285)

U.S. Consulate-General
Via leyetana, 33
Barcelona, Spain
Tel: 3199550
(or APO NY 09285)
(American Women's Club,
c/o U.S. Embassy)

Sweden
U.S. Embassy
101 Strandvägen 115 27
Stockholm, Sweden
Tel: (08) 63-05-20
Telex 12060 AMEBM S

Switzerland
U.S. Embassy
Jubilaeumstrasse 93
3005 Bern, Switzerland
Tel: (031) 437011
Telex 32128

Saudi Arabian Consulate-General
866 UN Plaza, Suite 480
New York, N.Y. 10017
Tel: (212) 752-2740

Embassy of the
Republic of Singapore
1824 R St. N.W.
Washington, D.C. 20009
Tel: (202) 667-7555

Embassy of South Africa
3051 Massachusetts Ave. N.W.
Washington, D.C. 20008
Tel: (202) 232-4400

Embassy of Spain
2700 15th St. N.W.
Washington, D.C. 20008
Tel: (202) 265-0190/1

Consulate-General of Spain
150 E. 58th St.
New York, N.Y. 10022
Tel: (212) 355-4080

Embassy of Sweden
Suite 1200
600 New Hampshire Ave. N.W.
Washington, D.C. 20037
Tel: (202) 298-3500

Embassy of Switzerland
2900 Cathedral Ave. N.W.
Washington, D.C. 20008
Tel: (202) 462-1811

Swiss National Tourist Office
608 Fifth Ave.
New York, N.Y. 10020
Tel: (212) 757-5944

Thailand
U.S. Embassy
95 Wireless Road
Bangkok, Thailand
Tel: 252-5040, 252-5171
(or APO SF 96346)

Royal Thai Embassy
2300 Kalorama Road N.W.
Washington, D.C. 20008
Tel: (202) 667-1446

Tunisia
U.S. Embassy
144 Ave de la Liberté
Tunis, Tunisia
Tel: 282-566

Embassy of Tunisia
2408 Massachusetts Ave. N.W.
Washington, D.C. 20008
Tel: (202) 234-6644

Turkey
U.S. Embassy
Atatürk Bulvari, 110
Ankara, Turkey
Tel: 26-54-70
(or APO NY 09254)

Embassy of Turkey
1606 23rd St. N.W.
Washington, D.C. 20008
Tel: (202) 667-6400

Turkish Information Office
821 UN Plaza
New York, N.Y. 10017
Tel: (212) 687-1530

United Arab Emirates
U.S. Embassy
Shaikh Khalid Bldg.
Corniche Road
P.O. Box 4009
Abu Dhabi, UAE
Tel: 61534/35
Telex AH 22229 AMEMB AH

Embassy of the
United Arab Emirates
600 New Hampshire Ave. N.W.
Suite 740
Washington, D.C. 20037
Tel: (202) 338-6500

United Kingdom
U.S. Embassy
24/31 Grosvenor Square
London W1A 1AE, England
Tel: (01) 499-9000
Telex 266777
(or Box 40, FPO NY 09510)

British Embassy
3100 Massachusetts Ave. N.W.
Washington, D.C. 20003
Tel: (202) 462-1340

American Chamber of
  Commerce
75 Brook St.
London W1, England
Tel: (01) 493-0381

U.S.S.R.
  U.S. Embassy
  19/23 Ulitsa Chavkovskogo
  Moscow, U.S.S.R.
  Tel: 2520011/19
  Telex 7760 USGSO SU
  (or APO NY 09862)

  Intourist
  16 Marx Ave.
  Moscow, U.S.S.R.
  Tel: 2036962
  Telex 7211

Venezuela
  U.S. Embassy
  Avenida Principal de la
    Floresta and Ave Francisco
    de Miranda
  Caracas, Venezuela
  Tel: 2847111
  Telex 25501 AMEMB VEN
  (or APO Miami 34037)

British Information Services
345 Third Ave.
New York, N.Y. 10022
Tel: (212) 752-8400

The U.S.S.R. Embassy
1125 16th St. N.W.
Washington, D.C. 20036
Tel: (202) 628-7551

The U.S.S.R. Consulate-General
2790 Green St.
San Francisco, Calif. 94123
Tel: (415) 922-6642

Venezuelan Embassy
2445 Massachusetts Ave. N.W.
Washington, D.C. 20008
Tel: (202) 265-9600
    (202) 797-3800

Consulate-General of Venezuela
7 E. 51st St.
New York, N.Y. 10020
Tel: (212) 826-1660

For a more comprehensive list of U.S. Embassies, Liaison Offices, Consulates General, Consular Agencies, etc. (some 280 in all), write to the Superintendent of Documents, U.S. Government Printing Office, Washington, D.C. 20402 and ask for publication 78777 "Key Officers of Foreign Service Posts" (price $1.50 for a single copy or $4.50 annual subscription).

For additional information about Foreign Service activities overseas or for specialized assistance with unusual problems, phone, write, or visit the Office of Commercial Affairs, Bureau of Economic and Business Affairs, U.S. Department of State, Washington, D.C. 20520, telephone (202) 632-0669.

Chapter 13

That's the Way It Was: Some Recollections

WHAT FOLLOWS ARE a couple of short stories to give you the flavor of what expatriate life can be like, but probably won't be.

Part 1

Idris Airport, in Tripoli, Libya, is not renowned for its amenities and expedient services. In fact, immediately upon my arrival in March of 1967, I found out first-hand how Libyan bureaucracy operated—very slowly! This was my first adventure as an expatriate and, believe me, I felt exceedingly vulnerable when negotiating with the baggage porter for the release of my luggage. "You very good man, *buksheesh?*" the bedraggled-looking Arab said questioningly. "Me carry bag to taxi, *min fadlak.*" There was an air of the military to his manner, and I suspected he was one of Her (or was it His?) Majesty's loyal servants during World War II. He struggled out of the humid, exceedingly grubby airport lounge—I use this term very generously, since outsized barn might be more appropriate—laden with three suitcases, a tote bag, and a suit holder. I walked behind carrying my passport and two bottles of Jack Daniels. The old man saluted, smiled graciously, exposing brown, uneven, mostly decayed teeth, and hastily pocketed the dollar bill I gave him for his trouble. "*Shokran*," he said, and was gone.

"Me no speak *Ingilizi*," the taxi driver drawled, shaking his head frantically.

"The Libya Palace Hotel!" I reiterated for the third time.

Finally, a gleam of comprehension spread across his face. "Five pounds, please," he answered, suddenly fluent in the Queen's English, "or fifteen dollars for you, very special rate."

Of course, I had no idea how far the hotel was from the airport, but a quick calculation told me that at an exchange rate of $2.4 to one Libyan pound I was about to be taken— if you'll excuse the pun—for an expensive ride.

During my carefree college days, speeding down interstate highways was exhilarating, and, on vacations to Europe, the narrow winding roads were challenging. This ride recaptured both, but somehow the exhilaration and challenge changed to unabashed fear. First of all, none of the roads from the airport into town were illuminated and so headlamps, on main beam, were apparently a must. A narrator better equipped to translate the outbursts of abuse that periodically erupted from my driver's lips—usually as he was struggling to get all four wheels back onto the hardtop—might have added more flavor to this rendition, but I think you have the basic picture.

To his credit, the driver was no slouch. We covered the twelve or so miles into town in about twenty minutes, having spent as much time off the road as on it. We pulled up outside the Libya Palace Hotel at about 1:00 A.M. It looked quite respectable from the outside and, since I felt thoroughly exhausted, I could not wait to take a hot shower and hit the sack.

"Sorry, sir, all rooms are taken," the young, rather arrogant desk clerk informed me before I had even put down my suitcases.

"Impossible," I replied, digging deeply into my jacket pocket for the confirmation slip, handed to me by our travel department just prior to departure. "Here," I said, thrusting the piece of paper under his nose. "One single room with shower reserved for Mr. S. Frith, confirmed 3/15/67."

He looked totally unimpressed.

"Sorry, sir, we have police convention, arranged very suddenly. They have taken all available rooms, *œsy*."

I looked at him in disbelief.

"Where the hell am I supposed to go," I asked him, raising my voice slightly and attracting the attention of a few late night guests, "at this time of night and with no reservations?"

"Try the Uaddan," he replied. "It's only a little way down the street. Out of the door and turn left. *Leloe saeida*."

If you have ever walked through a strange city, and especially an Arab city, at one o'clock in the morning with three suitcases, one tote bag, a suit holder and two bottles of duty-free liquor, not knowing where you are going, I don't have to tell you what an unnerving experience it can be.

Fortunately, the Uaddan was, as he said, just down the street. As I struggled closer, feeling like an overloaded pack horse, I noticed the doorman watching me closely as I approached. Not until I was ten feet from the front door, however, did he offer me any assistance.

"May I help with your bags, sir?" he asked, trying not very hard to remove the tote bag and suit holder from beneath my arms. I soldiered on, almost pinning him to the wall as I fought my way through the doors to the reception desk. If necessary, I decided, I would sleep right here in the foyer. This was the end of the road.

"Yes, sir, we do have a room," a youthful looking clerk answered politely in impeccable English. "It's on the fourth

floor, room number 414, but I am afraid the lift is not working. You'll have to use the stairs."

Out of the corner of my eye I observed the doorman beating
a hasty retreat back onto the street. The bell captain, I was
again politely informed, went off duty at one o'clock. Per-
spiration flowed freely down my face as I backed into room
414.

"What the hell do you think you're doing?" The voice came
from the darkened interior of the room. The accent was de-
cidedly British and rather pompous. The bedside light mo-
mentarily dazzled me, but soon revealed a middle-aged gentle-
man, clad in blue and white striped pajamas, sitting up in bed
rubbing his eyes frantically.

One would have thought after an indoctrination like that,
things could only get better, but during my three years in
Libya, a number of similar chaotic occurrences made it an
assignment to remember. Within two months of my arrival,
just as I was beginning to think that sharing a big villa on
the Mediterranean wasn't so bad, the Six Day War erupted.
Now, you would think with the Egyptian/Israeli front thousands of miles away, we would suffer little or no discomfort.
Wrong again. We were all subjected to a curfew from dawn
'til dusk, which I can assure you severely cramped the style of
four rather concupiscent bachelors. To be caught out during
curfew meant immediate arrest, or so we were told. On the
only occasion I ventured out—to get a case of beer from a
neighbor three houses away—a rather overzealous soldier
fired a warning shot (his words, not mine), which removed
three inches of plaster from the wall only eighteen inches
above my head.

Yet another fond memory I have of Tripoli is of one dark
night, about midnight to be exact, when an off-duty patrol
car raced out of a side street and completely wrecked my
sports car. Fortunately, nobody was seriously hurt, but a big
surprise was in store for me the next morning when I phoned

my insurance company. They informed me that the police records depicted the exact opposite of what I described, that I was, in fact, the one who ran a stop sign and hit the police car. It took the intervention of the colonel-in-chief of police to get that little mess squared away.

Six months before I left Libya in 1970, Ghadaffi and his troops executed a military coup that scared the pants off me. We awoke one morning to find soldiers all over the place, road blocks set up at every street corner, and radio Tripolitania politely informing us there was a twenty-four-hour curfew in effect. The airport was closed, and no communication with people outside of the country was permitted.

Despite the fact that U.S. Air Force Base Wheelus was on full alert and families were being evacuated into the base, many of us were asked by the company to help protect its property and make sure non-U.S. families of men who were working on drill rigs in the desert had enough food and water to survive the five-day, twenty-four-hour-a-day curfew. It was nerve-racking, stalking around the neighborhood at dusk, calling on families to explain what was going on and to ensure they had sufficient provisions.

Many of the Jewish stores in town were set afire, raging gun battles were going on all over the place between the army and the secret police (who remained loyal to King Idris), and tanks roamed the suburbs keeping a watchful eye on the expatriate community. It was a harrowing experience—probably the worst I have encountered anywhere on my travels.

Except for these irritations (and no air conditioning), my three-year stay in the Middle East was quite enjoyable. The Mediterranean afforded us an excellent means of relaxation and, within Libya itself, there are some fascinating Roman ruins and other places of interest. Since commercial entertainment (including TV) was virtually nonexistent, we threw lots of parties and enjoyed the great outdoors as much as possible. Tunisia to the west, Cairo and Beirut to the east, and

Malta to the north each had its unique characteristics that I could go on about forever—but I will spare you the agony.

Part 2

In 1819, Sir Stamford Raffles (after whom the Raffles Hotel, one of Somerset Maugham's favorite retreats, was named) founded a trading settlement on an island off the southern tip of the Malay Peninsula. In 1826 it was incorporated under a colonial government and remained the capital of British Malaya until, in 1959, Singapore became an independent state within the British Commonwealth.

I arrived there from the Middle East in 1970, and, within a short time, knew I would enjoy my stay. Sitting in the bar of the Singapore Island Country Club, sipping a cool beer and reflecting on a near-perfect round of golf, or singing ribald rugby songs with a bunch of Limeys and Aussies in the lounge of the Singapore Cricket Club after a very strenuous game of rugby is how I remember Singapore. It was a sportsman's paradise, and I recall that I played soccer, rugby, and golf at least once a week. Dining out was inexpensive, as were the discotheques and nightclubs. The social scene, unlike Libya, catered for all, and with a large expatriate community, we had a ball.

Although Singapore is an island, it does not boast good beaches; however, for a couple of dollars, you could hire a motor launch and spend the day at an adjacent island with palm trees, beautiful clean sand, and an ice chest full of cold beer. A causeway connects Singapore with Johore Bahru and the rest of Malaysia, and on several occasions groups of us would drive north on expeditions to Port Dixon, Fraser's Hill, Cameron Highlands, Mersing, Penang, Kuala Lumpur, or Malacca. Many of the roads penetrated dense jungle, and sometimes we drove for hours seeing nothing but an archway cut through the tropical forest.

In case you are wondering—yes, I did work. Singapore is a place where you work and play hard. The Asians are, for the most part, resourceful and hardworking people, and for expatriates to set any kind of example, an even greater effort was needed. Chinese, Malays, Pakistanis, Australians, British, and Americans all worked and played side by side. Singapore is one of the most cosmopolitan cities I have ever visited, yet one of the least race conscious. The annual rainfall in Singapore is about one hundred inches, and, while vegetation is luxuriant, the hot climate, because of humidity, is oppressive. With no seasons except for the monsoon, or rainy month, it is hot and sticky all year round and home-leave vacations were a welcome relief.

I left Singapore in 1973 and returned to the United States. A lot had happened in those three years on those 224 square miles of gateway to the Far East. I learned how to play golf (from twenty-four to ten handicap) and rugby, to water ski, to pilot an airplane, and to treat a snake bite. I got to eat real Chinese food, and I got married (to an English girl whose father was serving as a colonel with the British Army in Singapore).

Today I am located in England having spent the years 1974 to 1978 in our stateside headquarters. After experiencing firsthand what life was like on the Corporate end of the expatriate "hot line," my instincts compelled me to move on.

Next year, 1981, I will be in France.

In conclusion, let me say that I have experienced fourteen years of expatriate life. I have spent varying degrees of time working in England, France, Germany, Spain, Italy, Portugal, Nigeria, Tunisia, Libya, Egypt, Lebanon, Hong Kong, Thailand, Malaysia, Singapore, Indonesia, Australia, Argentina, Brazil, El Salvador, Mexico, and Canada. And I have visited many others. Each country was a unique experience for which I have many treasured memories (and souvenirs). Some places were better than others—the people more friendly or the climate less oppressive—but, as I said before, not all roads lead to Rome. Many lead to more interesting places beyond.

Index